I want people looking at these pictures to know that these aren't just ignorant little kids doing work. They are real people, and they have real lives and situations, and they aren't always as happy as they seem in pictures. Like, usually if I look happy, I am, partly. But there's always something at the back of my mind, so it's always more than what you see on the outside. There are problems and secrets that we all have. . . . Usually people will realize that, but not always. So, look hard. Sometimes it shows on the outside.

Christa Sanders-Fleming, Sixth Grade

Robert Coles

Nicholas Nixon

School

A Bulfinch Press Book

Little, Brown and Company

Boston New York Toronto London

Contents

First Edition

ISBN 0-8212-2501-4

Library of Congress Catalog Card Number 97-78282

This book is produced in cooperation with the Center for Documentary Studies at Duke University, publisher of *DoubleTake* magazine and DoubleTake Books.

Designed by Katy Homans

Bulfinch Press is an imprint and trademark of Little, Brown and Company (Inc.)

Published simultaneously in Canada by Little, Brown & Company (Canada) Limited

PRINTED IN GERMANY

At School
Introduction

The philosophical novelist and essayist Walker Percy was much interested in language, its defining and shaping significance for us human beings. Although a physician, he was not intent on a neurophysiological understanding of our use of words—the continuing scrutiny of the brain as the place where our thoughts take shape, our sentences get put together. Rather, he regarded language as an instrument of what he once called our "capacity, with another person, to arrive at various kinds of knowledge and perception." He was, with that statement, explicitly calling upon the work of Gabriel Marcel, the existentialist philosopher of the early twentieth century whose discussions of "intersubjectivity" became influential for many theologians and psychologists who have never wanted to forget Nietzsche's aphorism "it takes two to make a truth." Here is Dr. Percy reflecting on that theme: "Marcel was a religious thinker, maybe a theologian (though with no pretense to authoritative knowledge!), so he can be hard to understand—though what he was getting at, I think, is simple, in the positive sense of that word: the best kind of education takes place when we learn from one another and with one another—minds and souls in touch, rather than the individual standing apart and, as they say today, 'doing his own thing.' Marcel was, among other things, a playwright, and he understood how the acquisition of knowledge is mediated by the senses. We look hard and we listen long when we go to the theater, and, beyond that, the audience is a necessary part of what happens on the stage: it's a joint 'performance,' some of us might call it, a companionship—a 'chemistry' of the observer, on the one hand, sitting and watching and noticing and hearing, and the actors, on the other hand, moving and posturing and speaking in the constant recognition that there are people, nearby, in attendance."

I kept thinking of that statement, spoken twenty years ago by Dr. Percy in his Covington, Louisiana, home, as I accompanied Nicholas Nixon on visits to the three Boston-area schools whose children, whose daily lives, thanks to him, figure so tellingly in the pages ahead: the Tobin School in Cambridge, Boston Latin School, and Perkins School for the Blind. As I watched Nick, and watched children and teachers paying him respectful, affectionate heed, I began to realize that I was witness to a human connection, built and cemented over time—in Marcel's term, a consolidated "intersubjectivity," a photographer able and willing to have a heart-to-heart involvement, week after week, with youngsters in this or that schoolroom. Back and forth eyes went, and words: the photographer as an audience to the students, and they, in turn, his audience—their occasional mindfulness of him not an intrusion or an obstacle to educational progress but rather a stimulant to it. Indeed, I remember noticing Nick and two students in conversation, his head thrown back in a laugh, and their heads similarly extended, their responsive smiles evidence aplenty that this was a trio in eminently comfortable accord. Textbooks can be written, of course, about such a coming together of observer and observed—but at the time I thought my eyes and ears were the recipient of a scene thoroughly illustrative of what happens in the midst of sensitive, conscientious "documentary field work": trust given and received gratefully all the way around, an earnest, unstinting collaboration of minds.

Later in this book's text I will comment on the particulars of this impressive visual inquiry on the part of a photographer who has spent years chronicling children in their various and vital exertions of mind and body. Right now, I want to introduce a dedicated artist's hard-won body of work (all those months in such different educational locales within a particular city's metropolitan area!) and acknowl-

edge my gratitude: it was a real privilege to visit these schools with Nick and Bebe Nixon, to be challenged by what they enabled me to see and try to understand—young Americans of various kinds trying to come to knowing terms with their world's ever present and abundant mysteries. What follows are pictures and words: Nick's work with the camera; Bebe's work with the tape recorder at the Tobin and Boston Latin Schools (she earned the trust of ever so many children); the observations of a writer, George Howe Colt, who interviewed and observed children at the Perkins School; and, finally, my own comments, a combination of present-day observation and recollection of past work—a shared rendering of the complexities of schooling, a record for others to attend to.

Room 306,
Tobin School

John M. Tobin School in Cambridge, Massachusetts, was built in 1972 to replace a smaller, turn-of-the-century neighborhood school. It serves more than 750 students. In room 306, Nicholas Nixon photographed from September 1993 through June 1994 a combined fifth- and sixth-grade class that included his son Sam and was taught by Chris Affleck and assistant teacher Timothy O'Connor. Comments accompanying the following photographs are from interviews conducted by Bebe Nixon.

I can see it now. "Room 306: the average class, in the average school, in the average city, in the average state, in the average country, in the average . . . continent, in the average . . . etc., etc., etc."
Dana Jones, Fifth Grade

The best kind of learning is learning all together, in little groups or big groups; it's a really good way to teach kids. Learn with each other, not just alone. Kids who don't learn this way are really missing out. I think it's a privilege for us to be able to have this kind of education. People who just learn the traditional way, just by themselves, who don't get help, it's, like, totally un-nineties. It's also scary.

Julia Devanthery-Lewis, Sixth Grade

I think everybody's different on the outside, but on the inside we're just the same. Everybody on the outside has a different look, but on the inside, we all have bones, a heart, muscles, skin tissue, all that stuff. So everybody's the same, mostly. Physically. *But* in the way of behavior, I think I'm different from everybody. . . . I'm always like making jokes and stuff, saying things like, "Let us be cheerful while we work," stuff like that, because, you know, I don't want to grow up. Being a kid has been bad enough, so who would want to grow up?

Dana Jones, Fifth Grade

I really like learning about Greek myths. Different cultures are better to learn about, because in the beginning, you don't know anything about them, and in the end, you're pretty much an expert. I think knowing about those old Greeks changes the way I look at other people in the world today, definitely. You know, Lucien's from another country, and he's really, like, nice. And not everyone treats him really well. He's probably one of the nicest people in the class, but some people really resent him because they think he's too stupid to grasp things, because his reading and talking isn't that good. But it must be really hard, it takes a lot to come all the way from Haiti, or any other country, and to come to America and become so, like, fluent with this language. . . . It's hard and it takes time. I think learning about ancient Greece helped me see him differently.

Gene Damian, Fifth Grade

My mom says I'm one of those kids who's not afraid to go into something new, but just a little wary. There's been a lot of changes and stuff in my life, and it really has affected me, I guess. There have been some deaths, and people moving in and out. And people fighting in the house. And my stepbrother moved out last year, without even saying good-bye. So I'm really looking forward to having Chris again next year. . . . Because I don't want to go through another change.

Kim Richards, Fifth Grade

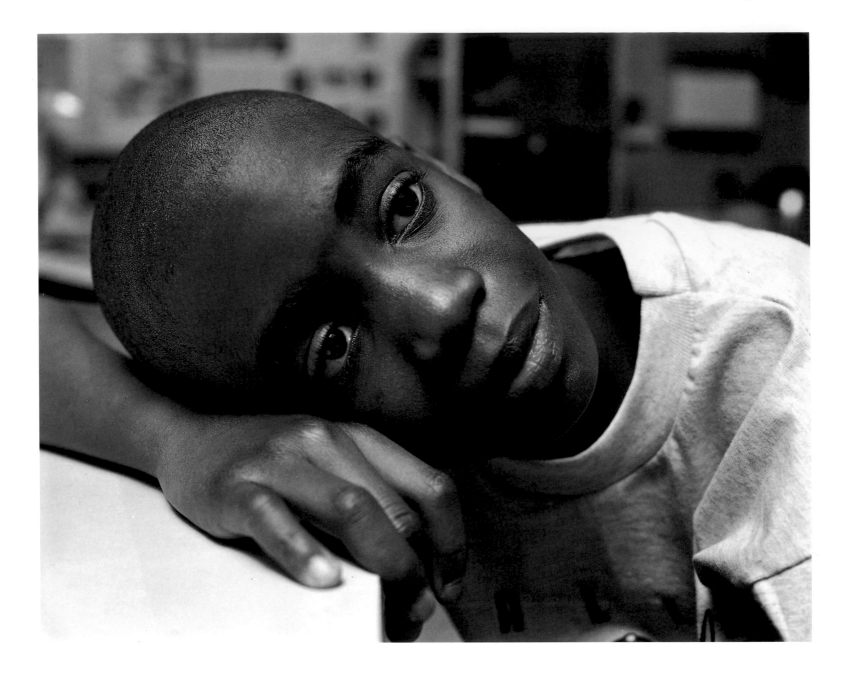

The pictures give a pretty good idea of the class, and how we are, except there's one thing missing. The teacher. She's not in the pictures. And I think she should be. Timmy, too. And Nick is *never* in the pictures. So that's not realistic, because he *is* in the room. Sometimes I think he takes pictures of people's feelings. Like when they're bored, and talking, or just sitting around, waiting. Or they're excited. The doves are in there. And he shows us working. Even though we do fool around a lot, working is what we do most, so that's the way it should be.

Robey Graham-Bailey, Fifth Grade

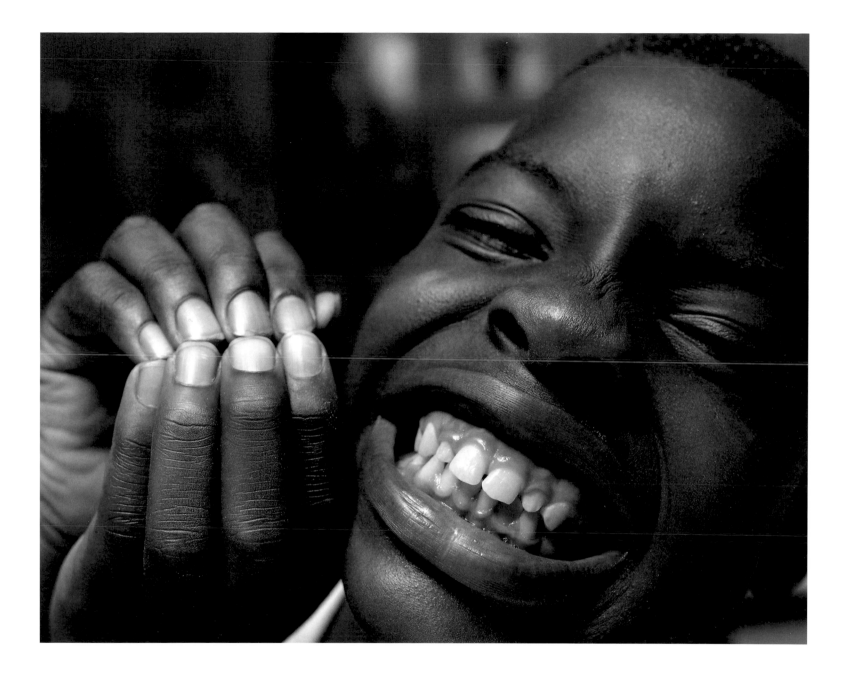

People like to say that men and women are different, that women are gentle and men are strong. It's not that way. There are plenty of boys in my class who, I know, would cry before I would. There are plenty of girls in my class that I know are strong in lots of ways. And, all in all, we can sit around together, give each other hugs, kiss each other on the cheek, hold each other, cry with each other, and still be the same as each other. And not think of each other as boyfriend and girlfriend. For me, that's not going to change.

Genita Mosely, Sixth Grade

The girls in the class are different from us. Chris kind of depends on them more, and I sort of take it as an insult. I think that boys can be just as trustworthy, but they don't just exactly *show* it. Their personality is to fool around. If they were called on to do something, and they weren't in a fool-around kind of mood, I think they could be fine.

The leaders in the class are Genita and . . . well, there are some other people who try to be leaders, but they try too hard. They try to lead the class, they don't try to be leaders. You know what I mean by the difference?
Sam Nixon, Fifth Grade

Feminism is an important part of my life. It's talking out and telling people that they're wrong. And telling people that things have to change, and that they have had to change since a long time ago. Feminism is . . . wonderful! I haven't had that much experience, just in school, but it's really important for girls to know that there is something out there that is standing up for you. And standing up for you when you get older. And that if you're having trouble, you're not just alone, there are a lot of people out there like you. It's almost a sense of community. It's not like you have to believe in everything they say, but it's like your *own* thing. If you believe in any part of it, then you're part of it. It kinda just grew into my life. Things that I said and things that I thought, even though I didn't know what feminism was, questions that I asked like, "Why can't I do this or why can't I do that?" If it wasn't for my mom then I wouldn't be the kind of person that I am.

Julia Devanthery-Lewis, Sixth Grade

A lot of people think I'm annoying because I cry a lot. Because I'm sensitive. And I've started crying less. That's a big change for me this year. I think as I get older, I'll start to cry less than I did when I was little. Last year I cried more. You get more mature as you get older. It sometimes means you don't show your feelings as much. I try to hold in the tears, and sometimes it's hard. I like being a sixth grader, except the fifth graders get easier projects. Sometimes I don't like being older.

Sarah Ritt, Sixth Grade

I know I'm going to miss this year. I'm going to miss the friendships and the kids. And everyone knowing each other. I think things are going to change when we go to seventh grade. I don't think it's going to change for the better, though. I think seventh and eighth grade are probably going to be my hardest years of education. There's a lot more kids, different kids, and we're going to be separated from each other. And there's not going to be any kind of time during the day when we can all get together and kind of . . . talk. I don't think I'm going to like seventh grade. At all.

Marc Riordan, Sixth Grade

A lot of times, I think I want to be an actress when I grow up, because I like acting and everything. And then I think, How *much* do I want to be an actress? I'm really interested in the Holocaust, so maybe I'll be a Holocaust historian. There are so many things I want to do, but I can't do them all. When I was younger, I wanted to be the President. But now I realize, I'm not into politics. Even though it sounds great and everything, I'm not into it enough. A couple of years ago, one of my friends did a survey of little kids, of what they wanted to be, and one little girl wanted to be a princess. And she's gonna grow up and figure out that she can't, and she's going to figure out something that *is* for her. When you're younger you only think of big important jobs, and only some people get to be those things. But there are smaller jobs that you can be equally happy in, and you get them, and you're happy. I'm probably going to change a lot, by the time I'm twenty, or whatever. So, I have no idea what I'm going to be, what kind of job I'm going to get. So what I'm going to try to do is, I'm going to write down everything that I want to be, make a long, long list, and then think. And wait.

Matisse Michalski, Fifth Grade

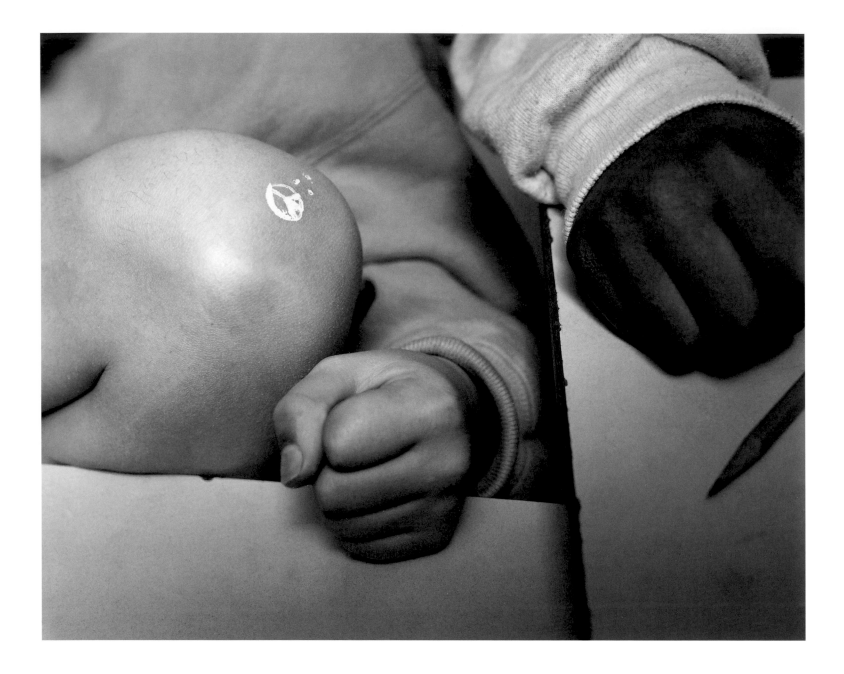

In Formation

They come into the classroom both excited and worn down by the bus ride—nine- and ten-year-old boys and girls in a combined fourth- and fifth-grade classroom of a Cambridge elementary school. For all the traveling they have done on behalf of their education they have yet to accommodate themselves to that fifteen minutes or half an hour of "start and stop, start and stop, and crazy noise," a shy Melissa describes it, and then a terse summary: "a wild time." Asked for amplification, she obliges, but again with forceful brevity: "No one [is there] to tell anyone to 'shut up.' " She would one day confide this daily yearning: "I get into the building and I wish I could find a place where I was alone, and there was quiet, so I could collect my head." A moment's pause and then a question: "You know what I mean?"

She is not, thereby, inviting a responsive inquiry that will, in turn, get her into an expansive description of what happens on those rides. Indeed, she directly challenges my documentary will: "The only way you can know what it's like is for you to be there [on the bus] in the morning, and then in the afternoon." A moment's silence is broken by a shrewd, knowing afterthought: "But if you were there riding with us, it'd be different." How different—and why? She smiles, shrugs her shoulders, tolerates an extended spell of silence, then throws out two words: "You know"—as if to remind this grown-up fellow that sometimes the obvious need not be spoken.

Yet, as we fumble for a new direction in a conversation, she has some second thoughts: "I'll tell you something—the truth is, if you came aboard [the bus] I don't think it would last long, the kids paying you attention, and so the quiet. Pretty soon, you'd be lost on them—the ones who get fresh. It's their 'free time' to 'act wise,' and *do* they!" Now she is getting excited. She imagines me sitting in the bus, has me get fed up, angry at what I'm hearing and seeing, and so, outspoken in an effort to calm things down. Then she conjures up a pointed response from an outspoken passenger: " 'Hey, we're not in school—we're *not.*' "

She has heard that refrain many times, of course—the defiant response of boys and girls both, to the bus driver, whose patience, finally, has been tried. As a matter of fact, she is willing to justify that assertion, bend over backwards to acknowledge its merits: "You see, a lot of folks, they have to let off steam. If they don't [do so] on the bus, it'll be building up in them, and there'll be trouble here in school. You see?" A nod on my part, however, doesn't satisfy her. She tells this eagerly assenting observer sitting beside her in a virtually empty classroom that he needs to see all right—for himself: "You need to go try it [riding on the school bus], then you'll get the picture."

So, I do, and though at first a visiting adult's presence does, for sure, exert a tempering influence, to the point that the bus driver is amused, grateful, delighted, in no time (three or four days) the new rider has become an "invisible man." Melissa noticed that outcome, and in another discussion, fueled by a shared experience, she ventures into the speculative territory of educational theory: "Some kids, they're troublemakers on the bus, but they quiet down once they get into school. They'll say they've got ants in their pants, and then they leave them behind when we enter the building here."

She goes further, bemusedly wonders whether "bus time" shouldn't be credited as "school time"; whether the first period isn't "on wheels"—the start of the day's learning. Pressed for amplification, she demurs. She admits to being "silly" regarding the observations she has just made—and now reverses herself, declares the minutes spent riding to and from school as "the opposite" of what obtains in a classroom: "When you enter the building here you've got to be different, and you know it, or if you don't, then you're headed for trouble, big trouble." Still, she is not quite ready to discard her notion of the bus as a place where something vaguely educational in nature occurs, the bus as linked to the classroom in some way: "First you're in your home, and you're not thinking of your lessons. As soon as I get on the bus, though—I'll remember what's coming up. I'll be thinking ahead. I'll be thinking of what we did yesterday and what we'll be doing today. I'll think of the kids in the class, and probably they'll be thinking the same thing, because we're all going to the same place. We're sitting on all those buses, and they're going to arrive at just about the same time, and there's a long line of them, and we're all stepping down and hurrying in (well, some aren't, they're dragging their feet real bad), and you can't get away from it: there's the school, and in a second you'll be inside, and it's different there, for sure."

When asked the obvious responsive question about the differences to which she alluded, Melissa shows a mixture of impatience and incredulity—surely a grown-up man who is a parent and a teacher doesn't need her to spell out what anyone with eyes and ears can quickly notice. But she obliges the inquiry in a more extended statement than her initial facial expression indicated to be forthcoming: "Once you've passed through the door, you're 'responsible for the rules'; that's what our teacher keeps telling us. You've got to remember that it's not just you here, it's everybody, and so you can't let your every wish decide what you're going to do. You've got to look around, and you've got to remember: there's the teachers and all the kids, and there are the rules, and you're one person, but there are lots of others, and that has to be on your mind, or else you'll cause trouble, and then you'll be in trouble, and when you're in trouble here, you carry it home, because they'll send a letter, or they'll call your folks in, and that way, you'll be hearing from your mom and your dad as well as the teacher. Once we're off the bus it gets quieter. The kids straighten themselves out: you have to get ready, or else you'll look messy, and the teacher might notice—in school, there's a lot of noticing that goes on!"

Her remarks prompt me to stand and watch and listen as the buses empty their human cargo. The boys and girls tumble out, glad to touch ground, noisy and restless. A few look upward at the sky, seemingly grateful for a sunny start to the day, or wistful in the knowledge that the sun will have traveled far when they next see it, or worried about clouds and what they have in store for the day. Of course if those clouds have already begun emptying their burden, the rain rules the talk, the actions of the children. They remark on what is happening; they huddle and hustle. They are pleased that they (or their parents) have had the foresight to urge rain gear on them, or they lament their lack of preparation, and take company in others similarly exposed, vulnerable, even as, alas, there are those who gloat in their own available protection, the leg up it gives them over others: "Why didn't you know it was going to rain?"

Not that the boy so addressed would take such a remark lying down: "I love getting wet!" Then, this: "You're a coward; you're afraid of a few raindrops!" But quickly both boys are silent as they approach a big brick building with big, black, metal doors swung wide open. They stop their ribbing banter, they glance at a teacher, busy in conversation with a child—who, ironically, has left her raincoat on the bus, and is worrying that she'll never get it back. The two boys, overhearing that, exchange looks, smile briefly—and then the joint impassive silence that Melissa had remarked on: two more contributions to a relative hush exacted by an entryway.

If there is a refrain, it is the word "later"—over and over it gets spoken: I'll see you later; I'll tell you later; we'll play later; we'll talk later; and, alas, such threats as I'll get you later, or just you wait and see later, or the word alone, the word itself, the powerfully compact sound a grim contrast to its extended promise of what the future will bring—*Later!* In a sense that word announces the renunciatory agreement virtually all the children have consented to make: when you go to school (and, literally, when you enter the building where classes are held) you agree to live up to that word "later"—to set aside one frame of mind, one set of emotions, in favor of another. To call upon Melissa, in this regard, one more time: "You know you've got to be your other person, your school person, when you're on the bus and on your way to that building. 'You put on your school person and do well today,' my daddy tells me sometimes when I'm being grumpy and I just want to go back to bed and to sleep and sleep; and he can tell, so he gives me that talk, and I say 'yes, OK,' but I'm not convinced, and he knows it. Then, when I'm getting off the bus, I'll hear him saying it, and by then I'm wide awake, and with all the noise on the bus, I'm glad to be putting on my 'school person,' and I'm glad the other kids are doing the same— they'd better or they'll be in trouble."

Not that an elementary school can command utter compliance with its rules of conduct. Nudging and poking and plenty of talk and smirking and giggling and some swearing and teasing—that is the daily stuff of the halls, the stairways, the corridors. With the help of Melissa and others I become conceptual, realize that there are five noise levels that can be discerned before my first class is actually ready to begin: the sounds within the bus as it arrives in front of the school; the sounds of the children as they approach the building; the sounds that fill the air outside the various classrooms; the sounds that I attend to as I watch the children sitting down, settling in for a long haul of another day; and finally, the sound (the absence of sound) I have to secure through a look, a gesture of my hand, a tap on my desk with a ruler, a vigorous clearing of my throat.

The start of a school day prompts a range of attitudes in the children before me. Some are ready and willing to begin the work of learning; some are reluctant or bored, indifferent; some are averse, wary, suspicious, ready in one way or another to fly off the handle. My observer-informant Melissa has warned me, however, not to conclude that these various postures are predictably related to the out-of-classroom behavior of the children. "Some of the noisiest kids on the bus are your best students," she once took satisfaction in telling me; and she insisted on telling me that the obverse also holds: "Some of the quiet ones, they're just keeping their powder dry, and they'll explode if something crosses them"—all in all a reminder of psychological complexity as it can defy our urge to make connections, assert correlations.

The eyes do, however, give clues to the teacher's eyes, or so I keep concluding. Many of the children are looking right at me; they are ready to go. Some are looking at one another, signaling messages known only to themselves (though I try to figure out what they are signaling). Some are staring at the ceiling, or gazing at the door, or taking in the window's light. I know that my voice will coerce a number of those wayward eyes, call them toward the rest of us who are beginning to form what is called a "class," but I also know that not always, even when things are going well, will all of us be attentively together. Indeed, some of the best students (academically speaking) have a way of stealing time off, or so I regard their ability to pay the closest of attention one minute—after which, they let their minds wander a bit, their eyes now glassy out of self-preoccupation. A privilege of their capability, their power, I have to remind myself as I struggle to make things clear to those who, in turn, are paying the closest attention, because they, too, are struggling to understand, to "put all the pieces together," as one of the students, Tim, who has a lot of puzzles at home, and loves to work on them, keeps putting it when I talk with him about his own experiences in our class and those of others (as he has observed them): "Some kids are whizzer quick; they get everything right away—they just put the puzzle together, all the pieces, as soon as they put their minds to work. Me, I'm slower—I have to think, and sometimes I'll even talk to myself: I'll say, 'Timmy, get to work, and pull it all together, and then you'll know what's the right answer, clear as can be.' There are kids who are really slow— you've got to help them with the puzzle. They don't get it on their own. My dad says you're not doing someone a favor when you solve the puzzle for them; but if the person is never going to get it another way, you have to pull some of the pieces together for them—help them part of the way— and then they 'get it,' the rest, for themselves (you hope)."

When he has finished he looks to me for agreement. I nod. He smiles, but soon thereafter his face clouds. He tells me that he worries on behalf of those kids who really need "extra help," even as he worries, in a different way, over the fate of the exceptionally bright students who are so fast on the draw in class: "If you're really slow you lose your confidence; if you're too fast you become a big, big deal in your own head. Either way, you're in trouble." So his mother and father have told him; so he has noticed. So he lets me know—but with a self-critical afterthought that takes me by surprise: "I guess I'd better watch out or I'll sound like a TV commercial for myself!"

This kind of appraisal of others (and self-evaluation, not to mention subtle or not-so-subtle self-admonishment) informs the first minutes of every class, I come to realize. The children are watching for what the teacher will pitch to them, but they are also gauging one another, wondering and worrying about themselves: who will catch what, and when? Even when they are working together, a team, each is the would-be recipient of the teacher's high fly or low ground ball, or, maybe, devious bunt. They never cease to be—well, *themselves,* as Tim is quick to remind me one day while we're discussing the various "teams" I've worked hard to arrange, so that the children would work collectively on various projects: "Even if you're all on the same team, you're still watching out for yourself. There are the ones who want to take charge, and some don't care if they don't do anything, and you get kids in between— they're 'half into' what we're doing and 'half out of' it."

Levels of engagement, of intellectual capability, of collegiality—so it can go in universities or elementary schools. I often had Tim's observations in mind as I chose particular children to work with one another, and so doing, noticed the children taking notice of what I had done—what I had asked of them before I put any explicit questions to them, or made any requests of them. Mostly they acceded in silence, but with grimaces or smiles, with a bodily gesture that signaled pleasure or pain. Sometimes, at the end of the day, a child would come to me, ask not to be connected to another child "too often," or "for a while, at least"—and then a story of woe, of bad blood, of anxiety or fear or envy or rivalry or frustration or humiliation: all the emotions to which we humans are heir. As Tim counseled once, in an after-school colloquy with his teacher: "You see [I didn't!], if you put Martha and Sally together, you're striking a match and throwing it on dried-up paper."

I didn't want to hear his knowing comment, his more than implied reprimand; so, I diverted us by wondering aloud about "dried-up paper"—what precisely did he mean by such a description. His face right away registered open surprise, disappointment, dismay: this big shot who can't face the facts, and stoops instead to literary analysis, a maneuver that deserves its own analysis. But he is patient, forgiving: "My dad says that if you let the newspapers stand around for a few days, they get drier, and they light up faster in the fireplace." He waits a second for me to absorb that, senses that I'm not persuaded, but wants to rescue both of us from this unnecessary distraction: "Martha is always on a slow boil, and Sally is cool, real cool—and they clash, they do. One gives the other a look that kills, and it just keeps happening [their looks, back and forth], if you have time to stay tuned into them! We all laugh when they have to sit next to each other [when asked to work together], but we don't show it [the amusement]. We figure, maybe *this time* it'll click, and they won't throw knives with their eyes; and we figure, you know what's right to do."

He is stunned by the implication of what he has said, which he fully realizes (so I realize). He tries to do an end run around this threatening impasse— tells me that the kids like the way I move them around in the class, so they're not always sitting at their desks, and so that they learn thereby to get along with the full range of their classmates, rather than those sitting (by alphabetical assignment) in this or that part of the room. "You should have your desk—it's like home," he avers, "but you should travel all over," he adds, eyeing me carefully, trying to discern if his pleasant platitude, meant to please, has taken sufficient hold. I decide, however, to pay him the compliment of confession; I tell him I sometimes *don't* know "what's right to do"—why I've tried to talk to the children individually, as we were then doing. I worry, though, as I say the above, that it's not smart of me to say such a thing, that I'm compounding my error all too markedly, once again

revealing that I don't know "what's right to do": a teacher ought not surrender his or her authority so readily! Won't children, under such circumstances, lose respect for this man or woman whose intellectual, psychological, and moral authority surely matters so very much, hence ought be kept thoroughly intact?

I try to have it both ways; I explain myself, hoping thereby I will buttress my standing in Tim's eyes, never mind my own—while I also manage to cling to my declaration of a flawed humanity. I tell the boy that I'm trying to learn, even as I teach, and I remind him that I'm a "volunteer," that my usual bailiwick is a nearby university. Tim is generously understanding, but not to a fault—he wants to uphold his original, sensitive perception about his two classmates, and in that sense, *his* authority as a young teacher (one who is doing exactly what I seem to be saying I need from the likes of him). He moves us along in this manner: " 'It's all right, you get to learn from your mistakes,' the principal said— they're changing the schedule we have, so it'll be better. Maybe it would be better, next year, if they separated some kids like Martha and Sally, so they wouldn't be in the same room. Then it would be easier on you teachers, and easier on us kids. Sometimes that's the only way—that it'll get better."

With that reminder of the limitations of any teacher's cleverness, ingenuity, we are ready to turn to the substantive matter of a boy's passionate interest in geography—his eagerness to learn the capital of every one of our nation's fifty states, his attentiveness to rivers and lakes and mountain ranges, to nations and continents and the oceans that separate them, his desire to know the numbers of people who live here, there, not to mention the sources of wealth that distinguish particular countries, regions. He has found a store where he can buy maps, and with the spare change that he gets from doing errands, and with the allowance he gets, and with occasional spontaneous gifts he gets from a doting grandfather, he has bought a dozen or so maps, which he treasures, consults—indeed, studies hard and long. Moreover, when a news story breaks on television, he is quick to look at the city or state or nation where a violent storm occurred, or a war began, a plane crashed. In the blink of an eye he can point out Rwanda or Burundi or Zaire or Liberia (or Libya); he can locate Bolivia or Bosnia or the Caspian Sea or Lake Lagoda; he can refer to such state capitals as Bismarck, North Dakota, or Jefferson City, Missouri. In that last regard, did I know that "if you write to the secretary of state" of each of our states, you can get the state seal—he is on his way to accumulating all fifty of them.

I am in the presence of a lad's great intellectual energy; I am learning how it informs his life in and out of school. I am being asked, actually, whether there isn't "some way" that Tim might be able to spend more time in subjects such as geography and history, less in mathematics—rather as if he were a college student, entitled to select a major and pursue it with all his might. On my face are doubts—not to mention the realization that a school's curriculum simply can't be shaped to each child's personal choices. The lad reads me fast and clear, responds to my mind's misgivings, its realism, as if I had spoken a long lecture: "I know what you're thinking: you've got to learn everything. I agree. It's just that—you could do that, only spend more time on what you really want to know. It would be 'special time.' Couldn't they have that [special time] for someone if he wanted it, and he could prove that he wasn't just faking?"

I am gripped by that last turn of his thoughts, and he somehow senses a heightening of interest on my part. The child becomes the psychological man, the worldly philosopher of resignation and realpolitik: "It's how it goes, that some kids will loaf around, or they'll take advantage of something, if they can. My grandfather, he says people are like that, but you shouldn't spend all your time worrying about them, because if you do, you're letting them be the boss."

Now I am hearing the unspoken—a boy embrac-

ing his grandfather's wisdom, but worrying that his teacher won't be fully persuaded by it. I am quick to nod, agree with the boy's presented argument, but indicate the practicalities of the case, to the point that Tim obviously feels defeat in the air. His body slumps, his head falls, his eyes look to a map he has been showing to me—as if, for a second or so he can have things his way. I yield, remind him (and, of course, myself) that there is "flexibility," that there are "study periods" we can put to good (and singular) use; and if (I move to the abstract) a student does well in his subjects, exceptions can be made—an arrangement of his time accomplished that will suit his abilities and his interests. Tim seems to fathom the reasons for my somewhat pompous recital of the obvious—a wry smile sent my way tells me we have gone as far as possible. Pointedly he takes us to Lake Lagoda—tells me that he saw on television a documentary on Russia's struggle against the Germans in the Second World War. Did I know that Leningrad (now St. Petersburg, he knows) was surrounded by the Nazis for two, maybe three, years, and lots of people starved to death, and the lake froze over during the long winter and that way some supplies were carried to the city on dogsleds? I had a distant knowledge of all that, but now I am hearing a historical story, geared to geography, chronicled in all its terrible details by an elementary school child who can transport himself and a listener across half a century of time, across the thousands of miles that separate Cambridge, Massachusetts, from Russia's second city, across the waters of the Charles River and the Atlantic Ocean and the Baltic Sea to the shores of a great lake whose use in wartime resistance had recently been conveyed to greater Boston's public television audience.

As Tim and I looked at a corner of vast Russia, I realized not only how much this subject matter meant to him, but how much he wanted it to mean to me. He had become the teacher, I the student. The duration of this shift in roles was up to me—I could encourage the boy to keep telling me what he learned, what I might profit from knowing, or I could find reasons to stop us in our tracks. I also realized how thoroughly aware this boy was of our present situation—even as he was telling me things, pointing things out on this large map, spread open on a table beside my desk, he was taking moment-by-moment measure of my mood, my level of attention and interest, the intentness, as it were, of my face, my body, as I heard him out, asked him questions. A teacher can tell a child (with a gesture, a frown, a pacing to the words uttered) that there is time aplenty or that life must move on—that enough is enough, and let's get back to that spelling lesson, or in this instance, the study period in session. In fact, three other children had been following the hushed exchanges between Tim and me, and I found myself, alternatively, worrying that we were distracting, disturbing them and wanting to invite them to join us—a seminar on a roll! For a moment I wished I could ask Tim to teach our entire class a geography lesson; that way, we'd learn about Russia's important cities, the water near them, and their overall importance historically, economically to a great nation—Tim's notion of geography was broad, deep, worthy of that subject as it is taught in certain universities, probably under rubrics such as "social geography" or "political geography." But I had no nerve, or if I had had some for a while, it had left me. I heard various rationalizations or self-justifications race across my mind as I concomitantly began to signal to my avid, zestful student that we had to conclude our time together—his mostly solo riff with occasional accompaniment by me: the others were growing restless, were feeling all too left out, and we had leaped into one person's quite private realm, which no one else wished to enter, explore (maybe even me, for all my show of wide-eyed, approving curiosity).

In no time an obliging youth took accurate stock of a classroom's educational, psychological atmospherics and was on his way to a full retreat: the map folded, the words diminishing in number and spo-

ken intensity, his eyes focused on withdrawal, on the safety of his seat, all the way across the room. Some of the children have been paying us no heed; they are preparing for the spelling bee we are soon to have—a suggestion of the children that I originally greeted with considerable skepticism, because I worried at the prospect of boys and girls reciting words (and, inevitably, words misspelled) in public. I'd been won over by the insistence of many in the class that they would learn better by reciting words rather than writing them down, and by the seeming absence of a lobby in favor of the traditional approach of a written test. A few children, however, had been keeping a close eye on Tim and me, and when he retreated to his desk, their eyes followed him—all except for one, a girl named Betsy, who was, alas, known as Mousy by some of her mean-spirited, full-of-themselves classmates, ready with ungenerous comments for anyone, everyone, or so it sometimes seemed to me on days when I myself was in a sour, and so, skeptical mood about the moral qualities in the youngsters before me. Betsy broke her glare directed my way to look at Tim for a few moments after he'd landed "home," but she was quick to include me, yet again, in her main line of vision, and do so in a rather unrelenting manner, to the point that I was anxious to ignore her look, busy myself with desk work—only to look up, and find my young observer steadily at work. I knew I was in trouble when I heard my mind calling up the word "Mousy" upon locking eyes with Betsy. If I were inclined to blush, I thought I'd have blushed; instead, I went back to my pen and paper chores, after glancing at my watch, noticing that all of us had five minutes before the bell announced a new "period."

Two minutes or so later, Betsy had had enough of my dodges; she raised her hand, and when I noticed her doing so—in a study period—I knew she was bound and determined in some way to challenge me. She did so with great tact, though; she came to my desk (she could have spoken from her desk, thereby making a public or class-wide spectacle of her remarks) and she whispered to me with the faintest hint of a smile on her face: "Couldn't we have a map lesson next, with you and Tim? We can always do the spelling bee some other time."

I was tempted to say nothing; to shake my head firmly; to let the matter drop there (while retaining for myself the right to regard Betsy not as mousy but as a bit of a rude or fresh young lady who ought have been taught long ago to mind her own business). But I knew I ought talk with Betsy, and I knew, as well, that we ought do so outside of the classroom. So, I stood, motioned her toward the door, while moving myself in that direction. Soon enough we had our conversation: "Is there something you wanted to say to me?"

"Yes"—but no more words, though her face registered a distinct wish to offer them.

Silence is a sign, maybe, that I had been perceived as not wishing to hear her talk, to give her permission to have her say. So, we stand there, both of us (all this in two, maybe three, seconds) digging in our heels—until, at last, I come to my senses, begin to comprehend my own anxiety: Betsy has something important to impart, and I have enough idea of what it is to not want to be told.

"Betsy, did you want to let me know something?"

"Yes, I did. I wanted to suggest—well, what I whispered, that we all look at that map with Tim and you; I mean with you and Tim."

"We have the spelling test (the spelling bee) coming up, and I can't postpone that without postponing other quizzes, and soon we'll be behind."

She looks at me, even as I'm wondering why I said what I just did. Come on!—I think to myself: we can work out all that test stuff! Aren't you the one, anyway, who wonders to himself and worries out loud to other teachers about some of the endless rote learning that goes on, to the detriment of the kind of serious learning that can take place when children are given a chance to make suggestions, take initiatives, explore subjects on their own or with the coop-eration of the teacher, even if they aren't on the school's agenda or curriculum?

"We could catch up, I'm sure we can."

She obviously wants to say more, she swallows her words—almost literally: I see her neck muscles working, she looks right up at me, and I want to turn away. I am, by now, ashamed of myself. For heaven's sake, why don't I greet this brave young girl as an ally, try to figure out with her how we might get a chance, one of these days, to look at some of Tim's maps, to learn from them and him—why am I so stubbornly resisting this idea, this proponent of it, and in the name of what? We are hardly on the brink of a radical educational coup d'état here! This student felt the warmth of a fellow student's intellectual fire, wanted to absorb it, in the company of her classmates. She saw me banking the fire, was saddened by the sight, gathered up a certain fire within herself, dared share it with me—and in return received from me some pompous, self-serving pieties: a teacher's evasion of a student's honorable, thought-provoking suggestion.

Abruptly, I do an about-face, both physically and substantively: I move us away from the classroom by a few steps, and acknowledge that the proposal of Betsy's is a good one, and ought to be pursued. I promise to do just that. I thank Betsy for bringing the idea to me, and I promise to share it with others in the class—and soon. She smiles, thanks me. Now her eyes are focused on the floor, as are mine. I start moving back toward the room. Betsy follows. Suddenly, she stops. I notice that, hesitate. We've got to get back, do our spelling work. But I can't leave her out in the hall. I turn. She looks right at me. She says, "Thank you" to me; then, she tells me this: "I wish I could own a map like Tim's. I'd put it on my wall with Scotch tape. My mom wouldn't let me use tacks, like Tim's mom lets him [use]. I'd have fun, learning all the places, like he does."

In no time we are spelling words, one person and then another. As I read out the words ("against," "decent," "consider," "generous," "investment"), I suddenly think of Tim, and ask him if he wanted to spell the names of some Russian cities on his map—and do so by writing them on the board. Yes, gladly—and so, in a short while we are all reading "Murmansk," "St. Petersburg," "Lake Lagoda," and hardest of all, "Vladivostok," which Tim calls an "easy one." Now I ask him for the map, and I look at Betsy, and I wink, and I'm ready to mount the map on our big cork bulletin board, but I'm suddenly moved to call her to my desk, and ask her if she'll help me. We proceed to do so with red tacks, which she obviously admires, and loves using. We eventually tell the rest of the class to come up, try to find the places Tim has called, and a few others I've mentioned, added to Tim's list on the blackboard—Odessa, for instance, and, of course, Moscow, and the Caspian Sea and the Volga River. Everyone is busy—some lost in the vast, mysterious expanse of Russia, others tracking down particular locations, still others feeling the map with the palms of their hands, as if thereby they were traveling over those enormous distances between the Baltic Sea and the Sea of Japan, between the Arctic Circle and the tier of Middle East and Asian nations on Russia's southern borders. "It's a huge country," one boy says. "Really huge," another fellow asserts. Then Tim and Betsy add their encouragement, tell the two classmates that it's quite possible to get to know the country, no matter its enormity—and with that reassurance, they roam far and wide with their eyes, focus on places, point them out to one another, then yield to another pair of their classmates.

Before long, an entire class had visited a map, come to know, with varying degrees of certainty, the approximate geographic contours of the world's largest nation, and, too, had developed a sense of its chief cities, ports, rivers, lakes—not to mention their spelling. An air of excitement pervaded the classroom—we'd trod a new path, enjoyed ourselves, learned a lot. Spelling had become linked to travel—even to history, for I told the children something about the czars, about the Russian Revolution, about

the rise of Joseph Stalin, and about his murderous Gulag. I also told them about Dostoyevsky and Tolstoy, and about Chekhov—and I showed them Sakhalin Island, where Chekhov, a doctor, made a study of the czar's penal colony: a short story writer's effort to describe how prisoners in a faraway place spent their days of confinement. I wrote the word "Sakhalin" on the blackboard, and beside it, the name "Chekhov." I asked the students to try to memorize the spelling of those two words, to stare them down. I pointed out the island several times on the map. I found a picture of Chekhov in a literary "dictionary," and showed the serious-looking writer-doctor's face to the children, who now wanted to know what else he'd written. I wrote the names of a couple of his best-known stories and of three of his plays on the blackboard. I spoke to the children about the stories and plays, tried to describe the rich psychological vein in them, the ironies they convey, the moral lessons a reader can learn from them. I heard myself talking too much, becoming too didactic—not the way to teach Chekhov, not the way to teach these children, and, maybe, not the way to teach. Still, the children were hearing my real interest in a particular author, and when I told them that my mother and dad loved to read Chekhov, and read him aloud to one another when I was their age, I quickly saw, heard, their unqualified attention—and right away, their hands were raised with questions. Did I listen when my parents read out loud? Did I read those stories or plays at that time? Could I have spelled Chekhov's name then? Were any of his stories assigned in school to me and my friends?

I leveled with the boys and girls; I told them that when my parents read to one another, my brother and I were "sometimes" interested, but often we couldn't care less—we wanted to play with our friends or listen to radio programs that told of "cowboys and Indians" or of "cops and robbers." Of course, our parents weren't especially eager to enlist our interest, they really were talking to one another, addressing "life" together, courtesy of novelists and short story writers whose fiction in some way stirred the two of them (gave them "food for thought" was the way I put it). I told them I probably wouldn't have known how to spell Chekhov's name when I was nine or ten, their age, or, for that matter, twelve or thirteen: we were never told of that great writer nor assigned any of his work, even through high school. Only in college did I "meet" him. The children picked up on that verb, wanted to know what he was like. I explained that he died in 1908, that I wasn't being literal. We had a detour there—now English was connected to our spelling and geography lesson! I asked them to use "meet" in the way I did—and a number of students did so quite well. "Today in class we have met Dr. Chekhov," Tim offered, and then the conclusion: "and he seemed very interesting, so we hope we can meet him again, and meanwhile we'll learn to spell his name right." Applause!

The students most certainly did learn how to spell Chekhov's name correctly, and, too, the island Sakhalin—I was amazed at how well they did with those words and other geographic ones. They looked and looked at what I'd put on the blackboard, and some committed what they saw to memory on the spot, and others wrote the places down for themselves on their notebook paper. Finally, I asked all of us, myself included, to put aside all "props," even as I erased the blackboard—to write down Chekhov's name, to spell Sakhalin and Lake Lagoda and Murmansk and Vladivostok. I pronounced each of those words carefully, and gave us all the time to respond on paper. The result: a great spelling success—even some of the students who did poorly in such exercises got most of those words exactly right. No one misspelled Chekhov, or Lake Lagoda, or Sakhalin—the words we'd examined most carefully, fully because of our class discussion. When I told the boys and girls the outcome, they cheered—not quite what they usually did after the results of a test were announced.

I mention that event of years ago because it was an important moment in my learning life—a time when a class showed what it could do (how it could soar) under certain favorable circumstances. In a sense, the rote learning of spelling had been turned into storytelling; and a teacher had acknowledged that a student's interests can sometimes prompt others to immerse themselves in a subject otherwise of no apparent connection to anything that's a part of a particular curriculum. Elementary schoolchildren are so willing, often, to break with routines, to experiment, to embrace the unusual, the exceptional, the risky. That morning, as we all got to know Russia at least a bit, I remembered a phrase used by a psychoanalytic colleague of mine, Selma Fraiberg—she spoke of the "magic years," a time when boys and girls of, say, nine or ten, are free to let their imaginations have relatively free rein, to the point, in this instance, that the children in my class certainly did "meet" Chekhov, and go visit his native land. I had the feeling, then and there, that I could have started to teach them the not-so-easy-to-learn Russian language; that I could have started a "social studies" class on the history and sociology of the Soviet Union, or present-day Russia; that, were I talented enough, informed and determined enough, I could have connected *any* of the subjects I was teaching to the Russia we had begun to consider—especially if I'd had some photographs to show the class, and, maybe, a documentary film, depicting various aspects of that nation's everyday life.

To be sure, we'd all experienced a "distraction"—and in time, with serious daily attention provided, Russia might fast become an obligation, a task, a burden, a bore. Yet, in all candor, I had to admit after the school day was over, that a child's energy had become infectious—and might well have kept prodding us, inspiring us for a good long time. Any doubts in that regard were put to rest the next day, when the children were quick to want to look at the map again, master some new geographic place-names, discuss Russian history, read Russian stories. When I heard myself telling them that we still had a lot of American history to get under our belts, and that we had no time to take from the planned curriculum for new projects, and when I thereupon heard their complete silence, saw their downcast faces, I knew the limits of my own teaching life—an inertia, a stodginess, a fearfulness, even, rationalized as a volunteer teacher's sense of professional responsibility.

Ironically, in my college and graduate school teaching I try to uphold the kind of free-wheeling, spontaneous, risk-taking manner the children were clearly seeking from me in vain—as in the use of James Agee's section of *Let Us Now Praise Famous Men* titled "Education," or Charles Baxter's story "Gryphon." I ask the teachers who take a seminar I give, "Writers in the Classroom," to describe some of the classroom challenges they have encountered, to connect their day-to-day experiences with the fiction or nonfiction we read. In "Gryphon," a substitute teacher (what I have been all along in elementary schools) whose very name is exotic, Miss Ferenczi, tries to shake up the students who eye her so eagerly, warily. She defies accepted routines, truths; is the flagrant rebel; and for a brief moment has her class almost ready to throw caution to the winds, follow her into a land of speculation, fantasy, bold, imaginative leaps. Unfortunately, she not only stirs the children, she scares them; she gets more than a bit carried away with her stories, explanations, interpretations (the way, perhaps, many revolutionaries end up doing)—and so the story is one of a daring dreamer come to naught. Still, her feisty originality, her idiosyncratic, visionary temperament strike a distinct chord in many of the boys and girls; they have not yet settled for the gradually imposed constraints of the status quo, whose accepted pieties have, of course, been successfully confronted only at a high cost by the likes of a Galileo, a Darwin, a Freud. It is far easier for most of us to go along, to get along; to make our cautionary peace with the principalities and powers of the respective worlds we inhabit, hence the persuasive worries that crossed my mind as those children pressed for a more adventuresome educational strategy: what about that list of words handed out to us teachers—why, we'll fall behind if I don't watch out! (I wasn't even remotely near Miss Ferenczi's state of mind—she who no doubt remembered the skepticism with respect to the conventions of spelling that writers as diverse as William James, George Bernard Shaw, Flannery O'Connor have in the past expressed.)

The children seemed to sense my timidity, maybe even the rationalizations and self-justifications I'd summoned in its defense. A girl named Janice, one of the quietest in the class, came up to me at the end of a day, two weeks after I thought we'd all laid to rest our spell of map-watching, to suggest a possible compromise, a way out of what she thought I'd formulated for myself as a dilemma: "If we could look at some of those maps, maybe we could do some extra homework, so it'll be all right." She didn't add to that sentence the two words I later realized she had in mind as she spoke, "for you," or "with you"—as if the problem wasn't really the desirability or the feasibility of a particular classroom activity, but the teacher's hesitancy, a fearfulness that needed to be addressed. I was struck by Janice's candid willingness to bargain with me—and on behalf of others as well as herself: "We've talked it over," she told me. In a full retreat, psychologically, I mustered the usual defensive ploys, a scrutinizing skepticism that has a slight paranoid tinge to it. "We?" The young lady was appropriately reassuring and tactful in her quick response: "Just a few of us, but the other kids heard what we were saying, and pretty soon there was everyone saying it's a great idea, and we should cooperate, so we could see more maps." I'm smiling now, and am brought back in my mind to that shared excitement of a while back: why not go back to it? Then, the old doubts—a distraction would consume too much time. But I say I'll think the matter over—and only with the encouragement of my wife, Jane, a longtime teacher, do I strike up an agreement with the children: we have to stay on schedule with our spelling if we're to venture into a new territory whose exploration will, inevitably, cost us substantial time.

A month into that experiment, it has become old hat. I can't for the life of me figure out why I'd hesitated, stalled, balked. What we do seems so pleasurable, rewarding, natural, *instructive*—to me, never mind the children. I'm learning about various countries, and, not least, I'm learning a whole lot of spelling—all those places we ordinarily recognize, vaguely know, but can't be precisely sure that we can write down accurately. Now, I'm expanding on this path, pushing it in new directions; connecting the study of maps to history, to literature, to art—telling the children what I myself had been prodded to do by this turn of events: pick up books that told me of discoveries, wars, victories and defeats, territorial gains and losses, the chronology of events that makes for a nation's story. I show them, too, slides of the cities we've been getting to know, of buildings and bridges and street scenes in those distant places. I read to them from the poets or novelists of those "far-off spots," as Janice so casually called them once while thanking me for "letting all this happen."

In fact, it was such an informality of language, so earnestly spoken, that conveyed the truth of what had taken place—we'd all been able to break free of certain intellectual and social inhibitions that have their own usefulness at times (the need for order, for adherence to a prescribed curriculum) but can also thwart students and teachers alike, deny them relaxed access to the kind of curiosity that can furnish a great energy to a classroom. "It's good to know all the stuff you're supposed to know," one of my fifth graders told me at the end of our experience with maps (the last day of the school year!) and then she offered this hard-to-forget qualification: "The only thing is, you can get sleepy by the afternoon marching all the time to orders. That's when you need a break, so you'll wake up." We went on for a bit—and as we did, I remembered that her father was a drill sergeant for a few years, until he got

himself into a military surveillance training program, and thereafter, membership in a radar maintenance facility. Later, talking about a class and its various members with my wife, as teachers do when the last class is over, and memories of a whole year are allowed to flood the mind, and thereby rescue from oblivion, at least for a while, all sorts of happenings, we realized how loyal to her father this girl was—not only in his life as a drill worker, but as an extremely close observer of the human scene.

Interestingly, the next year, when I tried connecting cartography with orthography—I got us all to learn and spell those two pompous words!—in a formal way as part of our regular and necessary work, the children were far less interested: they wondered *why*—and they noted that "others" (the two classes down the hall wherein their age-mates were learning their lessons) didn't "have to do that." When maps become a "that," when they become something that is regarded as compulsory, one more requirement handed down, no questions asked, no explanations offered—the result is acceptance all right, sometimes of a diligent kind, but not the lively enthusiasm that a child generates when he or she feels like a founding member of a particular prospect. In the second year of using maps I myself had gotten used to them, knew them better, had figured out in advance what I was to do, and why—hence a lessened excitement on my part, and a heightened sense of obligation on the part of the children. We were no longer side-by-side explorers; I'd taken the measure of one more educational landscape, and there I was, ever so sure of myself, handing out my binoculars to the children, so that they'd notice what I'd spelled out to be important.

Like the maps that tell of this or that world, the pictures that Nicholas Nixon took in room 306 of John M. Tobin School bring alive both pointedly and suggestively the elementary school moments teachers all the time are lucky to witness, even inspire. I know the Tobin School well as a commuting teacher who passes it by daily on his way to a university's classes, or yes, to do substitute teaching in Boston and Cambridge classrooms not unlike those of the Tobin School. That school itself, though, is relatively unique; it was built in the early 1970s, when the energy crisis seemed to be a lasting aspect of American personal and institutional life—a big impact on our driving habits, on the way we lived at home, on the kind of buildings we inhabited. The Tobin School was built to retain heat—its windows are few, its cement a massive presence: "the fortress" many Cambridge boys and girls call it. They go on to joke: "You get in there, you never get out"— just what engineers hoped would happen to the heat that is so necessary for those long New England winters. But once in there, the slabs of concrete disappear, yield to the rooms, their desks arranged in various ways, their walls covered with pictures, assignments, lists of things to remember, to do— and I couldn't help but notice, an occasional map, though none with the tacks and pins of many colors that my students so delighted in suggesting we keep using. But one mostly notices not things, but the young lives as they daily affirm themselves—a kind of energy generated not by oil, brought in trucks, but by young minds and bodies in constant action of one sort or the other. No wonder the teacher who oversees Nicholas Nixon's chosen room of learning (he spent months there, a daily, patient presence) tells me that she is "wasted by the end of the day just trying to follow all their actions with my eyes." I pick up on the verb "wasted"—which my own children loved using when they were younger, and which persists as an emphatic statement of exhaustion among the young, and now, their elders. The miracle of a photographer's chronicle, I begin to understand, is his own tirelessness—a strenuous commitment and endurance and agility, a constant readiness of response, in the face of such ever-present activity of mind and word and deed. These visual documents are a documentary record, then, of a late twentieth-century American elementary-school classroom as it came to persist in its unself-conscious ways, no

matter a tall, skilled man's watchfulness and his emblematic technological (objective) assertion of that kind of human subjectivity—the avidly inquiring eye become the camera's dramatic sequence of moments preserved for others to contemplate.

The dark-skinned boy peering, in one picture, over pages of printed matter just below his chin, echoes the photographer looking intently, a black cloth covering him and his notably present instrument of perception—the observer intently observed. To look at this picture is to be reminded how much teaching and learning has to do with sight as well as sound, the teacher's appearance, gestures, facial expressions as well as what is declared, asked—and, of course, the book's print, the blackboard's chalked messages, all awaiting the silent absorption that we call vision being exercised.

Of course, sometimes these boys and girls, like the rest of us, shift into neutral, so to speak, stop trying to get somewhere with their eyes, instead look inward, or gaze nonchalantly at nearby people, places, objects: a wonderfully content smile on a girl's face, her eyes just narrowed enough to protect her thoughts, perhaps; or a boy's head rested on his right arm as his wide-eyed stare allows for memories or worries or expectations or regrets rather than the physical and personal exertions of a room's immediate drama.

Even when others are attuned to the here and now, ready to seize a given day's moments, opportunities, possibilities, ready to surrender fully, willingly to its demands, some will resist, stare into their very own space with its own actions: let *them* raise their hands and take their stands, I have plenty to attend to that no one else can possibly find of interest. A girl in one of my fifth-grade classes put it this way: "I need a vacation for a minute or two every day here. I don't close my eyes; I just pretend to be thinking about what's going on, but I'm really a few miles away, having ice cream at my grandma's, or helping my mom cook supper."

So often, though, just about everyone is caught

in the action that accompanies, signifies, enables classroom education. Those above-mentioned eyes are thoroughly focused on a teacher, a book, the walls, the blackboard; those hands are raised, a prelude to a performance, an answer given, a question asked. Chalk is wielded. Books are held. Pens and pencils get used. Paper is marked, plucked from a clipboard or a notebook, set aside, filed methodically, crumpled, tossed in the wastebasket, or, alas, reduced to the size of a spitball (not in the Tobin School, maybe, but in schools where I've worked, and, long ago, every once in a while, in the genteel, suburban school I attended). As we see in these pages, children become actors, parade before their peers, make things on their own or together, hover over a page's words, their own words—or their drawings, or the objects they have crafted or assembled. They hover all the time between the known, the almost comprehended, the quite unknown. They touch one another on the skin—there are all shades of it, a welcome collective sight, in these pictures. They also touch one another in other ways—they smirk, strut, scowl, and not least, gently, encouragingly, smile! They take roles, wear costumes, signs. They assemble, huddle, strive as individuals and as a room's collective effort to make this or that point. They can be in awe before the arrival of knowledge, its formidable demands: numbers to be added, subtracted, multiplied, divided, the mystery of it all—the teacher a sorcerer and they his or her apprentices. "When I think of what you learn here, all of it—I just wonder who started this all," a boy told me after he'd at last mastered long division. When I asked him whom he thought was responsible for "all of it" that is out there waiting to become absorbed by him and others, he answered this way (thereby telling me a lot about his spiritual life!): "I guess God thought up arithmetic, and He gave it to someone, way back then—though I'm not sure God is a person. You see what I mean? My dad [he is a computer engineer] says Nature, everything that's alive—that's God. But how did we get smart enough to do all these tricks with numbers, and to invent computers? That's what I'd like to know!"

"To know"—every day's refrain in classrooms across the planet. Language is the defining characteristic of our species; it descends on us, and through it, we tell, learn, explore, invent: come to know and are known. In picture after picture these children are on that journey of knowledge, they are immersing themselves in factuality, making it their own, and they are learning from and about their neighbors, their fellow citizens, with whom they build, act, recite, converse, ponder and wonder and worry and occasionally argue hard and long. Under such varying circumstances—the continuing shift in each day as one lesson gives way to another, one topic or activity yields to another—children take on a host of responsibilities, and not a few roles in the theater of the day. One child paves the way, speaks up, becomes for a moment a leader. Others fall in line, gladly, hesitantly, or with no small reluctance. Still others refuse the company of the majority, even that of their teacher—withdraw into their respective worlds, and once there, smile or sulk or nurse grudges or make vows or wishes.

Once, watching a gifted elementary school-teacher at Martin Luther King School (also in Cambridge) do her teaching, I hear her try to pull an entire class together, round up various nearby exiles (self-imposed), refuseniks of one or another sort. She does so by repeating her requests for attention several times, thereby eliciting the most valuable assistance of her loyalists, who join her in directing their attention at the holdouts ("a child's stare is no mean thing," the pediatrician and poet William Carlos Williams once observed). But all to no complete avail—in corners of the room, I notice, stubborn outsiders go busily about their private affairs of the mind and heart. Finally, a book's crashing noise on the teacher's desk brings the last remnant of expatriates to their senses: their faraway looks get forsaken, their eyes focus on the two of us grown-ups—and then the eeriness of true rather than relative silence. The children themselves take such notice, await the expressed details of a teacher's obvious sense of urgency. But outside the classroom, on the street beyond and below, a truck's brakes wheeze, shriek, though not in time to prevent a noisy collision with a gnat of a car hellbound somewhere—and now a wreck. A spell has been broken in the classroom. The teacher looks toward the window, hesitates, lets go of her American history book and her own childhood volume *(Little Stories of a Big Country),* both hitherto clasped in her hands, and very slowly rises—as if pulled not to do so, but also prompted to go see, right away, what that "world elsewhere" has just experienced. She is not yet fully standing, never mind moving, when the last two children to surrender to her earlier demand for attention are up and at the window, looking hard at a city street's accident. They are soon enough joined by their teacher—while the rest of the class sits still, watching the three who are in turn doing their own watching.

I wonder why more of these obviously quite curious youngsters don't follow their instructor's lead, huddle near her to appease a quite human desire to see how others in obviously dire straits are doing. I realize, finally, that an irony has unfolded, that those hitherto least connected to a teacher's interests have now become her momentary companions, while the vast majority of a class that she has tried so very hard to bring together, to align with her intentions, has temporarily become a bit at a remove from her. After a minute or two she herself acknowledges what has taken place in the room, turns to the class, gives it an account of what has happened on the street, and anxious to be fair (a brief glance of hers goes toward the students who keep peering out the window) she tells the members of the class that they may come to the windows for "a few seconds." As the youngsters do so, the usual shuffling and pushing occurs—people fighting for a frontline view. All at once the teacher again asserts her wish for fairness—now by addressing the two who have been there at the window's

edge longer than anyone else, including her. But she speaks in general terms—not deigning to stoop to the particulars of the situation: "Will those who have had ample time to look please yield to others who have had no chance, so far?"

The two toward whom she has directed her request turn around to take the measure of her face—as if her words, in and of themselves, don't carry quite the authority she intends for them. She is quite ready, as it were, for them. She has been looking at their backs as she spoke, and now, as the pair turn, her eyes lock with theirs—it is as if the two of them are one, and she is herself becoming larger than life, morally. She emphasizes the extent and depth of her feeling not with further words, but by putting her hands on her hips, and not letting her attention, the line of her vision, at all waver. The two one-time recalcitrants, then privileged onlookers, perched in the best spot to watch people in distress and those (the police, other drivers, pedestrians) who have come to their side, get the message and heed it—make way for others, retire to their desks. Now, further irony, they are the sole students in the room who are seated, who are attending with some care to their teacher, as she, in turn, won't suspend her sustained scrutiny of them. Indeed, as the other children, sated by their time at the windows, begin to retire to their seats, the teacher seems almost annoyed—she no longer has these two toughly "independent" ones to herself. She gives us all a bit of a sermon, tells us that people "collide" (an obvious reference to the accident) when they don't obey traffic rules, pay attention to what others are (or should be) doing, often because such people are all too "wrapped up in" what they themselves are thinking or wanting to do. Then, the clincher: so it can go in school, as well—rules and regulations and requests get ignored or disobeyed by those who decide for their own reasons that they don't wish to comply, the basis of a classroom "collision," a counterpart to the automobile one just heard, then witnessed. For the first time, I notice, the heads of those two boys are lowered—even as the teacher has somehow managed to keep the attention of her class from getting diverted from her, turned toward the ones for whom the moral comments were intended. Quite a sensitive performance, I begin to realize; and she has, at long last, united her entire room of ten- and eleven-year-old boys and girls—even as, in room 306 of the Tobin School, a couple of miles away, I notice that her colleague similarly works constantly to hold things together, keep in line the potentially unruly, earn the graciously continuing regard granted her by those who clearly rejoice in her leadership.

I talk after school that day with the teacher from the King school—and learn that what I have prided myself all too much in noticing, she has not only perceived right away, but figured out how to "ride." When she uses that verb, I think of her as on a horse, leading the children on their ponies (one or two of which are decidedly stubborn, if not outright wayward). I ask her to amplify—tell her that it had been all I could do to keep up with what was happening, moment by moment, in that classroom, never mind have my wits enough about me to think of what I might do to take advantage of the quickly unfolding chain of events. She is quick to disabuse me of any notion I have of a consciousness constantly at a confident, knowing ready: "I have to tell you, that long ago I learned—well, at school the teacher is always the student, or should be prepared to be at a moment's notice."

She stops, seemingly satisfied that I have been told quite enough. But I want to be a further student of hers, even as, surely, I have just been one of her students. I look inquisitive, still anxious to understand—to know the extent of her awareness as she so shrewdly (with such seeming command of herself, of a particular situation) went about her job that earlier afternoon. Now she has to deal with me, the last of her students for the day—so she catches her breath, looks at my tape recorder with no obvious affection or even respect (so I decide as the slightest grimace crosses her face: *this* is what is responsible

for his importunate manner!), and proceeds to carry me through the steps she has just taken: "At school you're always on your toes, or you should be! A lot of the time I'm drawing on my gut as well as my head! I knew I had to corral in a few of my kids who don't give me much leeway—they're always 'testing, testing'! I try to do it 'gently, but firmly'—those are the words you keep hearing in the education courses you have to take, the psychology ones. It all sounds *right,* so *easy,* when you hear those professors talk like that, but you know, I've looked around, in *their* classrooms where I'm a student (I think one of the 'cooperative' ones!)—and I'll tell you: I notice some who are skeptical of what they are hearing, or they're 'off,' in some other world, or they're plain bored. God forbid that a teacher should bore her students. We're the last ones to know that we're doing that. I'm sure I fail to see myself as a tired bore, repeating herself in a dull, demanding way that plenty of the kids have no trouble picking up on."

She hesitates for a few seconds—as I think to myself that I am anything but bored now. She sees in a flash that I still want a bit of exegesis, a commentary that helps a pedantic observer comprehend an intuitive "moment" in an experienced schoolteacher's day—and so, she obliges: "I wasn't sure, at one point, that I was going to 'get' what I was after! One of those two boys is actually the 'smartest' in the class. I don't only mean that he does well in the IQ tests we administer (over and over!). He's a fast reader who understands what he reads—that's called 'reading comprehension.' He's got a great sense of humor—he'll smile to himself when he's reading, and often I'm pretty sure that I know what's so funny to him: some silliness in what he's reading! You could say that in a way he's too old for this class—way grown-up for it. He'll go to the library (his mother has told me), and he'll read books that 'adults' are reading, not 'children.' He pores over the newspapers there, at the library, and he'll ask his folks about what he's read. He reads the *New York Times* as well as the *Boston Globe!* But in class, sometimes, he's impossible—I'm tempted to send him to the doctor and the psychologist for possible ADD [attention deficit disorder]. He'll get 'difficult'—that's the word that will come to my mind. It's what my mother or dad said to me or my sister when we got 'out of bounds': 'You're really being difficult.' I've said the same to my own son every once in a while."

She abruptly turns silent just when I think she has a lot, a whole lot, to say. I wonder why. She seems for a second or two lost in her own thoughts. I want access to them, of course, but I say nothing. The best way, after all, to derail the chance that she'll return to what she was saying would be to intrude with a comment, a question. Let the quiet in the room last as long as it serves its purpose—I try to say to myself, even as I get a bit uneasy. This is not a clinical hour in psychoanalysis, I half register in my mind as I wait, and try to think of some casual remark I might need to make in the event of more silence than I can tolerate.

But words resume—a teacher suddenly becomes quite pointed: "I'm pretty sure I can handle those two, especially Larry [the boy she has been describing]. He's actually begging me, at times, for control, for firmness—and the worst thing for me to do would be to overreact. If I hold on to my 'cool'—I think I have, so far—then we work things out: he joins us, and at times becomes the class leader. The others know what I know, actually: that he's very bright, and it's hard to say—very strong and ambitious. He wants all of us to understand that he's someone to be reckoned with! Now, I know, some people would say that it doesn't do him any good in the long run for me not to confront him head-on, to crack down on him and his buddy Frank. I suppose if I sent them up for evaluation ('go the ADD route,' we say; you hear that a lot in the teachers' lounge!) —well, then we'd clear the air, and we'd be getting to the bottom of the problem. That's what a lot of people would want done. I know it. But maybe *I'm* the rebel, *I'm* the one who won't join the class and

cooperate [do as many of her fellow teachers would urge her to do, and would themselves do]. I'm trying to work with Larry and Frank in such a way that we respect each other: I've cut articles out from the *Times* and given them to Larry! I've meant them to be for the whole class, and asked him to pass them around—but I'll start with him. Each time his face lights up, and I know we're getting someplace. To tell you the truth, I thought we made some progress today, as well. I was gradually enlisting the interest of *everyone,* those two included. I *was* getting pretty tough—the way I should at times. [She laughs—a gesture on her part, those words, to her critics, including the part of herself that is in alliance with them!] Then that accident took over—and later, Larry was wonderful the way he talked about people who drive when they're drinking, or tired, or upset, or distracted, and cause trouble for others as well as themselves. It's too bad you had to leave then! [I had had an appointment with the school's principal and came back when the class had turned to an arithmetic lesson—and a quiz.]

"I guess I'm saying that the real test in an elementary classroom especially is your [teacher's] judgment on what the bottom line is with each of the kids you have—by high school, you can sort them out with more assurance. When they're nine or ten or eleven, though, they're 'in formation'; I like that phrase. A priest I know uses it all the time: 'our character is in formation,' he says—I guess he means it's not written in stone. I think I'm in a lot of trouble when I start making too many separations or distinctions, so that I don't allow the kids room to prove me wrong, or, better, show me a different side to themselves, an alternative picture! I know it takes a lot of work [to follow the advice she was just giving herself], and I fall flat on my face some days, when I'm tired, or I'm worried about something at home, or I've got a cold or something, and I'm just plain irritable, so I have no time to put myself through my paces—I mean, be as thoughtful and patient as I can be with those boys and girls. But you know what?

The *less* patient and thoughtful you are, the *more* work it ends up being—if I've learned anything, I've learned that. The kids pick up on you all the time, and if you give them the back of your hand with your voice—oh, sure, they'll become more 'compliant,' but they also clamp down."

She abruptly ends her long and interesting observations just when I want to hear more—the details of how they "clamp down." She can see what I'm after. She gets ready to oblige me, but then has some second thoughts. She looks at the clock on the wall opposite us, checks it out by comparing its message with that of her wristwatch (perhaps to let me know more pointedly that our time together has run out) and then starts shuffling some papers on her desk, in case I have become not only obtuse but rude—whereupon I begin to thank her for letting me spend so much time that day in her classroom, and apologize for keeping her after the children have left. She smiles, thanks me for spending the day with her students, invites me to keep coming back as often as I wish (this is my tenth visit) and gives her desk a final perusal before leaving.

I tell her I hope to return in a week, and ask her whether we might at some convenient time talk about "clamping down"—the way her students withdraw from active participation. She surprises me; she sits down, tells me she has "a few minutes," and becomes, yet again, articulate and reflective—and also, apologetic: "I'm afraid I may have misled you when I spoke like that—I don't mean that I say cruel things, and then the children become frightened, and don't say anything at all, because they're 'traumatized'! Far from that—I think I'm usually cheerful with them, or if I'm feeling 'down,' I'll tell them why, so they don't take it personally: I'll say I have a cold, or I didn't get much sleep last night because my husband got sick, and I had to take care of him. I'm not even sure you, as an observer, would spot the kind of trouble I meant when I talked about a kid 'clamping down.' It'll go like this: a kid will do something that catches my eye or my ear. A boy will tease someone.

A girl will be full of herself, get 'huffy,' my mother would say, and give someone a look of contempt. Part of me wants to keep my distance from something like that—children not being nice to other children. After all, if I got involved with every little incident I happen to notice, I'd stop being a teacher: I'd turn into a referee. You have to ignore a lot in a classroom; you have to remember that these children are still young, and they're just starting out, and they have a lot to learn about behaving themselves. On the other hand, you can't *underestimate* them! You have to expect a lot of them—that they master the subjects taught them, and that they learn how to get along with each other, and, needless to say, with us, their teachers.

"I fail, most often, when I don't take advantage of a moment—when I see a boy not living up to his ability, or a girl just getting by, when she could be way out in front, and I just let the matter drop, because I'm under the weather or my mind shifted into neutral, and I'm just coasting—like the kid I see who is *also* coasting! Then (you know what?) I'll give the kid a look that says you're goofing off, and I know it, and I'm disappointed in you, and I'm sure letting you know that right now. It's all in a look that I give the boy or the girl, and you may think I'm exaggerating, but these kids know me and I know them, and a lot that goes on (maybe the most important things that happen)—it takes place in silence; it's written on my face, in my eyes, in the way I move, and the same goes for the kids: we send signals and receive them.

"Don't get me wrong—no one falls apart! There's no public scene! But the kids can tell when I'm not up to snuff, and they show it: they are just a bit slower, less eager to go that extra mile, more likely to be irritable with each other, because I'm a little irritable myself. They'll see me looking irritable, or they'll hear irritation in my voice, and they get impatient with the kids they know best, or the kids they trust enough to show their feelings. On the other hand, when I'm 'up'—they sure follow my cues. They shine, they glow with their behavior and their answers to my questions—we have a lot of fun together! You know what one of my all-time favorite students said—she was in my class two years ago: she insisted that when we're all 'going great guns,' then she remembers what we study better and longer. She was being tactful; she was letting me know that a teacher doesn't only impart information, and a student doesn't only prove on a test that she has learned the lesson correctly—it goes way beyond that: you can teach kids to take what you're saying to heart, and keep it there, or you can teach them in such a way that, sure, they'll memorize something, and write it down, but it's in one ear and out the other, and I mean it, I know the difference by the way they speak, and even the way they write, especially on the English or the history tests!"

She was, actually, showing me by example what she meant—she was speaking with intensity, conviction, and I was thoroughly attentive. She gave me a number of examples, anecdotes—a chronicle of lively moments in an elementary school classroom, times when the children got excited by a lesson because the lesson was interesting, in and of itself, but also because she had gone out of her way to enliven the lesson, connect it to the children's life or her own in a manner that really worked. She and the youngsters thereby went beyond memory work, beyond lists and requirements—found themselves on a terrain of mutual respect and affection and trust, helping and handing one another along. Under such circumstances, learned obedience gives way to considered initiatives spontaneously and gladly suggested, encouraged, fulfilled. It is then that new ideas are offered, considered, put into words. It is then that hands are raised not in response to being called, but out of a child's wish to explore, to move a class into an uncharted, yet inviting, landscape.

A last, summarizing moment that afternoon went like this: "You don't need that machine [a nod toward my tape recorder] to 'study' a class. You need only your eyes—why, you could stand outside a classroom, with the door closed, and in a few minutes you could figure out the whole story—the truth of that class. All you need to do is look through the window at those faces; and watch how the arms are raised; and see the way the kids look at each other and at the teacher, and how the teacher looks at them; and let yourself scan the room, see how it's decorated, whether there are plants, or maps, or pictures, or a small library for the boys and girls to use. Some rooms in this building look so *cold* to me—I shudder. But I remember days when I'm feeling lousy, and for all the warmth in my classroom—all that I've done to brighten up things, to make us all feel cozy—there's a pall over us, because there's one over me, and it's infectious!

"When a day like that is over, I feel so disappointed in myself—not in the children, but in me: the lost opportunities of a Monday or a Wednesday! I've sat here in this chair, and I'm wiping away tears, and if someone asked me what's wrong, I'd be ashamed to tell them, so I'd make up an excuse. I'll be going back in time, thinking about what I should have said *then*, and what I should have done right afterwards. I'll be cringing at the mistakes I made. Yes, yes, we're none of us perfect [I had tried to be reassuring with a polite banality to that effect]; but if you know better, and you let the right chance slip through your fingers, then you end up empty-handed, and you feel bad."

She stops for a second to tell me that she's not satisfied with the way she just put the matter. She is being trite. She expects her children to be original-minded, and there she is, summoning worn images. Once more I try to indicate my immense satisfaction with what I am being told—an astute, dedicated elementary schoolteacher self-critically conveying to me what makes a classroom work, or fall far short of what it might accomplish. But she seems to be addressing the very matter that I want to ignore, or refute as inappropriate: "When I stop being self-critical, when I keep finding excuses to justify my past actions, then I'll know it's time to retire"—so she tells me with a clear insistence that won't brook any interference. For a second I hear my mind's all-too-available psychiatric and psychoanalytic language rally to my defense—by going on the offense: she has this or that "problem," and the result is an unfortunate inclination toward self-incrimination, self-recrimination. But she is ready for me and my kind; she tells me that the best classes have followed her worst—that her failures teach her. She puts in a plea for self-scrutiny and reminds me that she keeps asking the children whose education she is trying to further whether they have tried to learn from their mistakes. This is a fifth-grade teacher, I finally begin to realize, who favors intellectual reflection and moral introspection in herself and in the children sitting before her in that class; and a teacher who gives those youngsters credit for being quite up to such a task. "The whole world is there, at the call of those ten- and eleven-year-old children," she reminds me, reminds herself—hence the challenge, but also, the solemn responsibility: "So, you have to hold your breath and live up to this wonderful moment in their life, and in yours: this time of openness, these years of scouting and leaping in the dark and speculating and sending up trial balloons—before things get fixed and certain." With those words, she is ready to leave for the day—though not without a sweep of the room, by her eyes, as if she wanted to absorb its memories once more, take them to heart as she said good-bye to a job, but also a calling.

Boston Latin School

Founded in 1635, Boston Latin School is the nation's oldest educational institution. It is a public six-year college preparatory school that provides a rigorous academic program in the classical tradition. Approximately 400 students are admitted each year on the basis of a competitive entrance examination. Beginning in 1974, in response to a court order affecting all of Boston's schools, a quota system was established that included setting aside places for minority students. Nicholas Nixon made the following pictures in 1996, in the wake of a lawsuit filed against Boston Latin and the Boston School Committee on behalf of a twelve-year-old girl who had been denied admission despite having received a higher examination score than students admitted under the quota system. That system was dismantled; a subsequent plan slightly favoring children poorly prepared by the Boston school system was also challenged in court. Comments accompanying the following photographs are from interviews conducted by Bebe Nixon.

63

I knew nothing about the Latin School when I came here. I'd never heard of it until my assistant principal came into my sixth-grade class in East Boston and asked who wanted to take the Latin School entrance exam. And you know, at that age, everybody's just looking all around at each other, seeing who's doing what, who else might go down to the cafeteria and register, and I just stood up. . . . It sounded good. I get to get out of class, let me go downstairs and check it out. There were no more than five kids who stood up . . . a white girl who was a friend of mine, and another black boy. Definitely no more than five kids . . . but some of them looked like they knew more what they were doing, more than I did. So I registered. And I came home and told my mother, "Ma, I'm taking the Latin School exam. You have to take me over to the Cleveland Middle School on, I think it was, Saturday, November second." And she said, "OK." Here I am, this little sixth grader, taking this big decision on myself. I've always chosen my schools myself. I told my mom I didn't want to go to a local school when I was in kindergarten even. I wanted to get on that bus and leave the neighborhood, Dorchester. I'm not sure why . . . there's always been something about being close to home. It wasn't for me. I'd gotten the experience of the neighborhood, and I wanted to experience someone else's. And I'd get a better genre of kids, or students. And of course there was the fascination of getting on that bus and getting out, even as a kindergartener. It was the greatest thing. I'm the first in my family to come here.

Rashaun Martin, Class I

I went to a Catholic school, and we all came from the same kinds of neighborhoods, same kinds of families. And of course we all wore uniforms, so the only visible things about us that were easy to remark on were our shoes. And I was literally being judged by the shoes that I wore. We were all constantly being judged, graded, measured. . . . And when I came to Latin, the whole world opened up for me. You were competing with people on all kinds of different levels. There were so many opportunities, just in terms of other people who were so talented: they had so much to offer me, just as individuals. . . . Just the conversations that happened, the interactions, just in general, were so valuable to me. . . . When I got here I found that I came from one of the most diverse backgrounds of anyone.

Marianne Staniunas, Class of 1996

Latin was one of the most tumultuous courses. Everything depends on the teacher you have. My second-year teacher really lit me on fire. She goes to Rome every summer, she has this passion for Latin and for history, and I picked that up and I really love it now, too. And I've learned so much, not just the stories, but of course they're great too, but about the poetry, and Vergil, the *Aeneid*. They try to build up Rome as this great civilization, and it's the epitome of everything, and I look at that and I look at their faults, and I learn more about how we could learn from what they did. In trying to build up Rome, I see the shortcomings of our culture. . . . And the language itself, at first I thought I could never learn it, I never believed I could look at this stuff and translate it, make something out of it, because there are so many different rules, not like English, or Spanish. Spanish I could do, that was easy. But Latin? You mean there are different endings for this, that, and the other, and you have to memorize all that, and there are different cases? Why can't they just speak like us? And also, they don't end their sentences. They don't use periods, they just keep on going, and so in a test you'll get, like, five lines, and it's all one sentence, and the subject is up here, and the verb is way down there, and it was just too convoluted for me. Then I got this great teacher. I didn't even really like her that much, but she was just so strict, and so demanding, and so rigorous, and every day she made us work and said, "You're not going to get a good grade in my class unless you really work hard every night and sit down and learn this." Because of her I was really able to understand how to translate Latin. And ever since then I've loved it. I like doing my Latin homework now. It's like a puzzle, and now that I've been able to translate it on my own, I learn a lot from what the stories are saying, and where to put what.

Melissa McClinton, Class II

77

Sometimes people in the school, teachers, get this image of you, and they stick with it, even if it's not who you are. My friend Pedro, he has this image as a slacker, a kid who does no work. And I know he's smart, but because of this idea the teachers have of him, they don't expect anything of him, so he kind of fulfills their idea. I'd really like to help him prove them wrong, but it's really hard to get out of that rut once you're in it. The first impression you put on the teacher is really important; if they don't think you have ambition, they won't change their idea. . . . Because I have this way of not paying attention, people, kids and teachers, have this idea of me as someone who doesn't work hard. Even when I do work hard. I don't get much sleep. After my homework is done, sometimes it's eleven-forty-five before I get to bed. A lot of people here don't get enough sleep . . . like Pedro—he has baseball, he has a job, he has homework, he goes to bed at one or one-thirty. I have to practice my music, do exercises for my back, and of course I have to spend time eating, taking a shower, being a normal person. Teachers always seem to forget that.

Vinh Truong, Class IV

Having . . . diversity was absolutely one of the finest things about my education, if not the most important thing. And I have to believe that there must be some way to avoid losing that. I think we're looking for solutions too quickly, trying to resolve the situation right now, once and for all. Like what they did with busing, get it done and over with, we'll make a decision and that will take care of it. What a lot of us ended up advocating was . . . keeping the quota system intact while you went out to aggressively change education on the lower levels. But it's not easy for politicians to get behind. . . . It's not glamorous, it doesn't make headlines. . . . And they can't get the credit on the front page tomorrow.

Marianne Staniunas, Class of 1996

There's this stereotype that all Asian people get good grades. That's not true. I've seen that not all Asian kids get good grades . . . and that not everybody who's from a certain race goes a certain way. I've seen that. It's really helped me to expand my mind about life in general. At first, about the Asian kids, when I thought they were all really smart—and I had this idea that that was just the truth, because of this prejudice I had in my mind—when I started seeing things that didn't go along with that, at first I just didn't accept it. I just really didn't know any better. Now, I know better. I have friends who are, like, homosexual and bisexual, whatever, and I can just accept them for what they are, not, like, what society puts out there, which is that I should stay away from them. I've learned to accept people for who they are as a person inside, not for what they look like or what their sexual preference is. I'm an extreme extrovert, very outspoken, I try to do my best and help out with whoever needs help, even if it's not my culture.

Naima Abdal-Khallaq, Class III

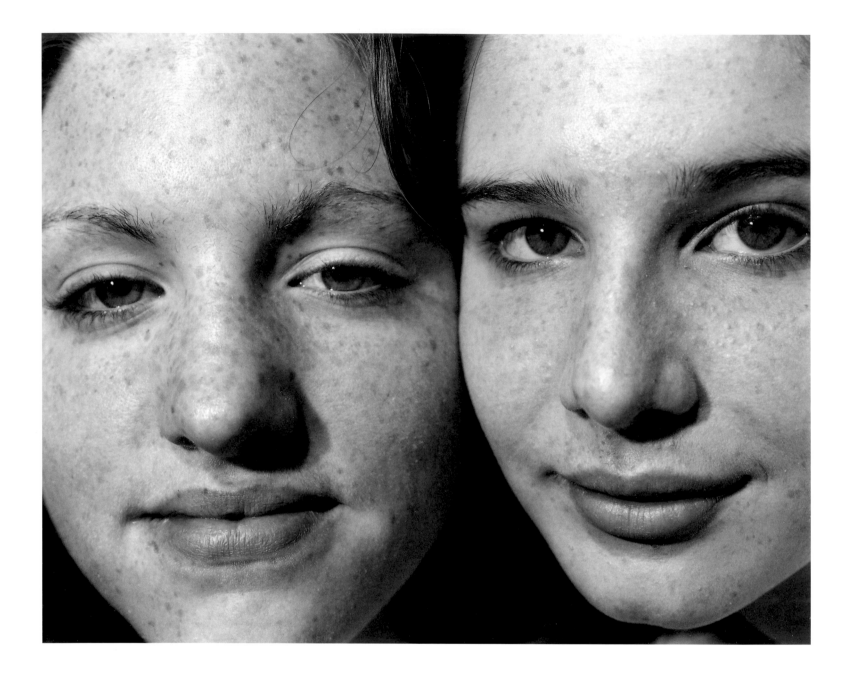

This summer I'm going to work at the Attorney General's office. I'm kind of debating about doing a double major, in political science and psychology, because I want to do something worth doing. I know I can't change the whole world, but. . . . I definitely don't want to be a politician, because I don't want to be a liar. But I do want to be president of my class. I'm not going to be good about getting up there and saying stuff I don't mean. That's why I don't want to be a politician, because I don't want to turn into someone that I'm not. And I don't want to get swallowed up by a job, where I wouldn't be happy.

Naima Abdal-Khallaq, Class III

95

How They Sort

In 1630 the Pilgrims landed; in 1635 the Boston Latin School was founded—and a year later, Harvard's life began: an important decade in America's history. America's oldest public school would give the nation Samuel Adams, John Hancock, Benjamin Franklin, Emerson, Cotton Mather and Santayana, not to mention hordes of businessmen, doctors, lawyers, professors. For over three and a half centuries young Bostonians have hearkened back to the Greek city-states, to Rome—learned the discipline of a classical education that mandates Latin (and, these days a miracle of sorts, encourages Greek) and, as well, offers a curriculum strong on literature, history, higher mathematics, the sciences. All the while, those students, almost every one of them, have gone to America's finest colleges. Indeed, in the early years Latin School graduates almost routinely crossed the Charles River to attend Harvard—and still do in substantial numbers.

Until this second half of the twentieth century all those graduates were men, and, almost all, white men. I was a student at the school after the end of the Second World War, and I recall only one or two African-American students in the entire school, no students from Spanish-speaking families, and very few (maybe three or four) Asian-Americans. The school began with Class VI, the seventh grade—so, for six years, until we became members of Class I, just about all of us were Catholic, Protestant, Jewish (or some of us, a mix of the aforementioned), and

from white, middle-class families. We were admitted to the school by competitive examination, or on the basis of our elementary school academic record. Some students came from outside the city, paid tuition. We all intended to go to college, and did—in those days an exceptional characteristic for a student body, and actually still so, if one considers the great expanse of America's public schools. Yet, we were curiously unaware of the above—that is, we went about our intensely studious ways with little recognition or acknowledgment of how lucky we were, how privileged. The emphasis was on duty, obligation, responsibility, obedience—the school's corridors were quiet, its classrooms silent, save for the teacher's voice, or that of the student he had asked to recite. Our desks, bolted to the floor, were lined up in rows. We wore coats or sweaters and ties—compulsory dress. The first letter in our last names determined our place in the classroom. All teachers (they were all men) got called "sir." We were called by our last names. We stood while answering questions or reciting. We saluted the flag every morning. Many teachers insisted that we hear the Bible read every morning. Caught whispering, we were given "misdemeanor marks." Caught cheating, a student was censured, "expelled."

In a sense, then, a public school had the authority of a private one: the right to set standards for admission; to refuse those who didn't measure up, as determined by tests; to dismiss students, pronto, for violation of various rules, regulations. No one was admitted or denied entrance on the basis of social standing or race, religion, ethnic background. A young man of whatever ancestry who did well in schoolwork and in tests could come to the school, prosper, graduate, and proceed to a good college. Young women went to the Girls Latin School, across the street, where the same principles and practices, ideals and requirements obtained.

In recent decades Boston has changed, and, unsurprisingly, its schools as well, including the Latin School. There is no longer a Girls Latin School —the Public Latin School, always the institution's official name, now has both men and women as teachers, students. Even as substantial numbers of African-American families and people from Puerto Rico and Latin America began arriving in Boston after the Second World War, their children increasingly became a part of the Latin School's student body. Not as prominent a part as many would wish, including many of the school's teachers, but therein a complex story. If a school's mission, worked into its history, its very name, is to further the classics, academic excellence, and if it has opened its doors to all who have shown themselves able to perform exceedingly well in the standardized tests that have such a hold on the entire range of American educational life (including our colleges and graduate schools), then how to make sure that more and more minority students attend such a school—if selection is "color-blind," in that it is done by test scores? Some have argued for a selection that takes race into consideration; others have insisted that the elementary schools that minority students attend be strengthened, in the hope that more of those boys and girls will perform better on the all-important qualifying or entrance examinations. Still others have questioned the authority of the qualifying tests, the stranglehold multiple-choice exams have on our contemporary educational life. Meanwhile, the school has tried to increase the number of its minority students—sometimes bypassing white applicants in favor of such students, even if their scores on

those entrance examinations are lower. The white parents whose children are thus denied admission to the school feel aggrieved, and one parent recently went to court, got a favorable judgment. In a significant historical irony, the same federal judge who prodded the Boston schools mightily a generation ago to desegregate (through busing), and so doing earned the wrath of many white parents, and, yes, some black ones who preferred neighborhood schools for their children, is now the judge who has recognized as an inequity the fact that students who have done well on the entrance examination get passed over, while those who have done less well are granted access—and, alas, to complicate matters further, some of those who haven't done well on the examination haven't done well once admitted to the school. The big question, then: fairness for whom—calling, that is, upon what moral (and social and cultural) criteria?

The old school has in many respects become a new school, even as it insists tenaciously that it is wedded to a particular intellectual tradition—and it is the photographer Nicholas Nixon's distinctive achievement to have given us a visual sense of how the past and the present have very much accommodated themselves to one another, and, thereby, every day, make for a future surely all its own. On a blackboard Vergil's dramatic initial (and initiatory) declaration that begins the *Aeneid*'s lyrical narrative is being written ("Of arms and the man I sing . . .") by an informally dressed African-American woman of studious mien—and there it is, the historical continuity of a language and a school as they connect with the last years of this second millennium: the civil rights struggle in obscure Southern towns, soon enough become the North's call to battle. This young woman's demeanor, at once casual and intense, her ability to give Vergil his due in her own accurate and relaxed way, tells a lot about a school's ability to hold fast, yet tack graciously, honorably in response to history's winds. So with another blackboard scene: those famous "moods" that have (in English, Latin, Greek) challenged generations of ever-so-properly dressed white "boys" continue to pose their challenge—here mediated by an obviously resolute, earnest (woman) teacher of color whose students are responsively attentive, no matter their at-ease appearance. Another blackboard scene bears eloquent witness to a school's tradition of intellectual seriousness, as it has persisted over the centuries: John Adams's shrewdly knowing characterization of generational commitments, responsibilities, possibilities hovers over a present-day classroom's vitality, of which not the least evidence is the spirited exchange taking place between two students whose differing racial backgrounds and genders seem, now and at last, utterly inconsequential, given their shared and obvious eagerness to understand a given subject matter. Finally, two youths more formally attired sit before another blackboard—the young man, for all the world, one of countless students who attended the school ages ago (the glasses, the shirt and tie, the well-scrubbed appearance) and the young woman, in her attentive elegance, a reminder of what a school, a city, a nation, can take for granted: hope become flesh—where once there were the grim prospects of servitude.

Other pictures in this series bring us close to the everyday rhythms and rituals of a school that continues to take quite seriously scholarship in all its forms. A young woman works on the always challenging mysteries of the Greek language. A young man for a brief second lifts his eyes from a paper that has been engaging him—and despite the message on his T-shirt, he seems headed for success. A young woman stands to recite—and through the window to her back one can see nearby Simmons College, a view that has been available to generations of students, many of whom went to a school different for sure in its student body and faculty.

Then, there are the more pastoral moments in a Latin School life: students aiming for music rather than classical languages; students sitting beside one another, daydreaming, maybe, or thinking of matters personal rather than academic (though the sign above them warns us not to "read" their minds);

students taking a break, their arms on a shared desk, a girl's faint smile directed at a boy whose eyes have their very own angle of vision; and, not least, two pictures that attest to the shifts, the complexities of a school's days—a head put on a table for a moment's rest, a head resting somewhat on an arm, a head's attention given a book or (perhaps, in the forefront) a teacher, and, at another moment, students all looking at someone, something, while a well-used book, a crumbled paper on top of it, assumes a powerful, summoning, telltale authority: the sometimes tense demands that can, inevitably, strain the nerves even of the dedicated.

So it now goes in a school whose survival is no small miracle in a world so bent on change and more change. Boston's Public Latin School is still outstanding in its capacity to prepare young minds for college, connect young minds to the learned wisdom of writers, historians, scientists, shape young minds in such a way that they welcome rather than fear the thinking life. To be sure, an atmosphere of achievement (required by teachers, attained by students—or else!) is not without its considerable psychological and moral hazards: arrogance, smugness, a constant, frantic competitiveness, a wearing of the nerves, a hardness of the heart that go hand in hand with the inevitable fight to stay afloat, to court victory. Yet, we see in these pictures much evidence of a humanity, a goodness of manner and being in constant assertion, and therein the heart of the matter: students gaining respect for one another as well as for the education they are acquiring, not to mention for the school's teachers who are offering it to them; and all of that become learning for the viewer, courtesy of a talented, determined man who carries an awkwardly large camera, and who disappears under a black cloth to snap his pictures—a hooded photographer stalking a school's truth.

As I looked at those pictures of today's Latin School, I remembered some of the elementary schoolchildren I've come to know in Boston's various neighborhoods who have gone to that school, found it ever so congenial to their interests, capabilities, aspirations, or, alas, a great challenge if not burden to bear. To begin with, the school attracts students citywide, so one meets people who live on streets miles and miles away, and, not rarely, from a different background. "We have lots of different kinds of folks in Brighton," a fifteen-year-old Latin School youth tells me—then the contrast: "But in my classes now there are kids from parts of Boston I've never seen, or even heard of—it must be like that in college: folks from all over." He would gradually get to know his own native city through cafeteria and hallway conversations with young men and women from those different (and often quite distinct) neighborhoods, and he would, as a result, read the newspaper differently, pay attention to television stories he might otherwise have ignored, because Hyde Park or Dorchester or Mattapan or East Boston or South Boston or Charlestown or West Roxbury or the Back Bay or Roslindale was now identified in his mind as a place where particular individuals live whom he had come to know; they, like him, traveled across Boston to get an education. In a sense, then, when he arrived at the school, he learned about new regions of his native city as well as a new language, spoken thousands of years ago in a distant part of the world.

In time, that language, Latin, becomes the basis of a new neighborhood, a means by which a diverse group of young people can gather together in mutual recognition. Here is how this young man, Alan, describes what has taken place: "I was in the Chestnut Hill shopping mall, looking for some sneakers, and hanging out with my old buddies [from the street where he grew up, who were going to the local school, Brighton High] and I saw this guy, and he had a BLS jacket, and at first I was a little embarrassed, because my buddies say I'm all right, because they know me, but Latin School kids are 'nerds,' and they're 'stuck up,' and they're 'nuts,' and they're this and that. But I knew I'd seen that guy someplace, and we said hello, and he told me he's from West Roxbury, and he was there to get some shoes, and we talked about school stuff, and I

thought, What the hell, I'll introduce him to my friends, and I did, and we went and got ourselves a snack and we hung out together for a couple of hours, going from store to store, and just looking.

"It was funny, when we came to a bookstore, my buddies laughed, and said they'd wait outside, and my Latin School friend and I should go in there— 'That's your kind of place, the two of you.' I said, 'Hey, no'; I said Latin School has nothing to do with it—so we all went and browsed. The next thing—the guys [his 'buddies'] asked us if we were going to look for Latin books. I laughed, and so did Mike [the other Latin School student]. But we got into a 'pretend' argument—the guys telling Mike and me they bet there were some Latin books somewhere in the store, and Mike and me saying 'no way.' So, to prove it, we asked one of the salespeople, and she looked at all of us as if we were 'way out in left field.' Then she saw Mike's BLS insignia [on his jacket], and she assumed we all were from there, and the guys pretended they were, all five of us now, going there, and she said she could order any book we want, if it's in print, and have it for us in two weeks max, so my buddies said, 'Go ahead, Al, order something.' I told the lady no, I wouldn't. As we walked away, Mike said he was tempted to order Caesar's *Gallic War*, just to be a big shot, but he didn't want to spend the money, and why order it, when you get it free to use at school! When we said good-bye to him, my buddies said, 'He's a regular guy, just like us.' 'What did you expect?' I asked—and did I get an earful! It's not fair, how people rush to conclusions on the basis of something like where you go to school!"

Such an observation lends itself, of course, to a larger discussion—the manner in which race and class and place of residence can also persuade various people to "rush to conclusions." This young man grasped that point on his own because of experiences like the one just described—not all of his neighborhood friends were willing to overlook his decision to go to the Latin School. Right away some of those youths "drifted away" from him, and not always with the kindest of words in their minds, on their tongues: "When I hear about the black people experiencing prejudice, I think to myself, You don't have to be black to get called names. A lot of us who go to BLS had to take the same kind of mean talk from people we'd known all our life. It's what one of the [BLS] teachers called 'a common denominator': you're called 'stuck-up' and names like that—worse, to be truthful. (I don't think you'd want to hear them!) If I'd known I was going to go through that, I'm not sure I'd have signed up. I mean, my mom and dad were in favor, all in favor, but even they were upset when they heard what—what I was hearing. It came as a big surprise, and it took a long time for me to get my hide tough, so I could just laugh and not be bothered. When people say they want to know what it's like to go there, to Latin School, I tell them the first thing they should know is what happens once it gets out that you're intending to enroll. Before you even step into the school you've been branded by the kids you've known all your life—and you know what? You're branded by their parents, some of them, too!"

A student of a particular school is giving a lecture on psychology and sociology; he is rendering out of his own experience what the writer of fiction, long and short, Tillie Olsen, tries to evoke in her piercingly brilliant story "O Yes," one of four that make up *Tell Me a Riddle*. In the story black and white children soon enough figure out how race helps shape their respective destinies. The author italicizes the phrase *how they sort,* a refrain of hers meant to remind us of a certain inevitability in human affairs. In similar fashion my young informant was giving me a vivid report on the telling consequences of attendance in an old and excellent high school. The ambition and intellectual capability of the young men and women who get a carefully designed and implemented classical education do not escape the notice of their friends, or, for that matter, their relatives. Inevitably, alas, envy, rivalry, and their sometime consequences, resentment, bitterness, begin to appear in many ways, large and small. These days, of course, we tend to emphasize the question of race—

how many African-American students attend a school known not only across Boston, but all over the United States. Yet, class as well as race bears down on all of us, boosting some, lowering possibilities for others—and, needless to say, there is always the matter (as James Baldwin once put it) of "class within race": the "sorting" that takes place, for instance, among families who belong, or aim to belong, in E. Franklin Frazier's well-known phrase, to the "black bourgeoisie."

Years ago, when I was working with African-American children in Boston's Roxbury neighborhood, I got to know well a youth, Geoff, who proudly attended Latin School. He worked hard there, did well. He had a fine way with words, and hoped one day to be a journalist. (In fact, he would go to Harvard, then its law school, and is now a corporation lawyer.) He idolized Arthur Ashe, and taught himself how to play tennis—hours and hours spent in a city-run program. One afternoon, as we talked about his studies, his great interest in Cicero's orations ("a real smooth politician, that guy") and his abiding affection for "hitting the ball, hitting the ball over the net," we got sidetracked into a larger discussion of his (and my) "alma mater." Geoff caught himself, actually, in a moment of "arrogance" in connection with that phrase, and that self-critical episode prompted no small amount of remembrance, reflection: "I think that when you go to a place like that [Latin School] you have to watch your step, or something happens to you. Hey—a lot happens to you, obviously! I have to laugh, when people talk about 'racism,' and how it works so that blacks aren't in BLS (as many as 'should be'). Well, I can tell you stories of what happened to me when I told people I was going to Latin School, and what has happened to me ever since I've been there—and I'm not talking about 'racism' at BLS! 'Who you think you are!' That's what I've heard a million times. I try to keep a straight face. I even lower my head a little—play at being Mr. Humble himself! But they keep on teasing me, or joking about my 'big-shot' ideas for myself. I've figured out ways to keep my cool—you rise to the bait and you're *through!* When I hear 'Who you think you are?' I correct the question in my mind to 'Who *do* you think you are?' You know what that is, though—that's me being 'uppity.' That's me turning my back on my own people—trying to be some 'house nigger,' talking like the white folks do in the mansion on top of the hill!

"Don't smile [I obviously couldn't keep from doing so]—most of my friends have never seen BLS, and they actually believe it *is* that 'mansion on the hill.' You know how I know? They'll ask me if I spend a lot of time 'looking down on where we live here,' and I tell them no, no, I can't see hereabouts, where we live, from there, where Latin School is [situated]. But they won't believe me—they think it's a skyscraper, and it's on top of a hill! I tell them it's only three lousy stories high, *three,* and it hasn't much land to its name, and all you can see from the windows is some buildings that belong to a college or two, that's all, and the land is flat as can be, and nearby is a busy street, and you have to wait and wait to get across it, but they don't want to hear any of that. They laugh and say 'yeah, yeah!'

"If it's my friends, we somehow get around the business—they end up believing me, or they stop kidding me. But I'll tell you something: there are kids here (I grew up with them, I've known them all my life)—kids who think I go to some place that's 'a honky palace,' they'll call it, and it's on some huge hill, so folks can look and see wherever and whatever they want! You're the doctor, you tell me if they really believe it, but they sure seem to mean it, when they say it, and they're not 'horsing around' or 'fooling around'—they're dead serious, and on their faces I see anger, plenty of anger. It's as if I'm 'honky, the boss man,' or I'm headed that way: the lines are drawn!"

Those remarks were part of a longer disquisition on Geoff's part—an attempt of a high schooler to fit his own life into some social and cultural as well as racial perspective. When I heard him talk, I was reminded of the trials I witnessed in Atlanta—as African-American high schoolers struggled to initi-

ate desegregation during the years 1961 and 1962. Some of those young men and women had to contend, of course, with the skepticism, if not outright hostility, of many (but not all) of their white classmates. Harder for them (so they said) were the mean-spirited comments directed their way by their acquaintances and neighbors in their own community, a reminder that, to call upon James Baldwin once more, "there's plenty of room for irony in Negro life, as much so as in the white world." Indeed, he made that remark to emphasize the refusal of some civil rights activists to see his people as anything but victims. He wondered why; indeed, he wondered whether such an attitude bespoke more than plain ignorance: "I'm afraid that some people who are on our side in this terrible struggle are profiting off us—I hate to say it: we're their 'cause,' and they see all of us in that blanket way. I suppose the needy should forget all that and just be grateful—but I'm afraid some of us aren't made to be *that* generous!"

Not that plenty of African-Americans, like their white counterparts, don't rally to the Latin Schoolers among them—and not only for reasons of family loyalty. The same young man, Geoff, who could so tellingly describe the subtleties of class (and of individual psychology as it gets connected to class), was able to remark upon quite another aspect of the human condition, as he came to observe it: "I was in church the other day, and the minister called out my name. He said I was working hard, and I was going to 'one of the best schools in the whole United States of America, a school second to none,' he called it, and so I should stand up. Well, I was so damn embarrassed, I wanted to sink through the floor to the basement below, or slip out and run fast, fast as I could. My mom knew what I was thinking, and feeling—so, she patted my hand, and she whispered, 'Please, let him enjoy himself talking like that.' She was being so smart, my momma! The fact is, that guy gets all carried away with things—and with himself! My mom was telling me to play the whole thing down, and she was right, so I did. But you know, my closest friend was there, and he and I are like blood brothers. He's the brother I've never had. [He has five sisters, all older.] Afterwards, we went for a long walk—a couple of hours. We ended up in Franklin Park [a large expanse of recreation land that makes all the difference to many who live in a nearby neighborhood]. He kept on saying that it's 'ridiculous,' the way people give you 'an automatic A in life,' and keep congratulating you, just because you go to a school. I was really glad to hear that—but then he got tough with me. He said that I've got to expect all that I get, because I'm asking for it—to go there, to Latin School. Wow, did I lose it! I flew into a rage: way out! We can trust each other, so he took it for everyone who's thrown stuff at me, and I've been silent, 'quiet as a lamb.' I became a screaming tiger. I said *give me a break*—I said that in fifty different ways! I was shouting. We were near the golf course. Some guys turned, and I could see: they were worried. But I kept going, until I was emptied of all words."

He can see that I want to hear some of what he said. He shakes his head, ostensibly to indicate how angry he still feels, in thinking of that afternoon, but also, I speculate, to let me know he isn't going to retrace his steps, this time with someone surveying the territory at his side, not to mention making a record of it all. I respond to his nay-saying head with a nod of mine; I speak—I tell him of memories that won't let go, of the book-filled green bag I brought home, the wisecracks directed at me, the one carrying it: a 'grind', 'a bookworm.' He smiles, says he's heard 'that'—though put more insultingly. I tell him I have long forgotten some of the insults that were tossed in my direction. He wonders, now, whether we both aren't making too much of what we've experienced, feeling sorry for ourselves. Look at what people have gone through in this world, he remonstrates with me, with himself—and then, the irony: he mentions the struggles of young blacks to desegregate Southern schools, because he knows that I came to know many of them in the course of the research I did during the 1960s. I decide to share

with him some of their experiences that I found exceedingly hard to hear of, never mind describe for others. I let James Baldwin do the initial speaking for me, just as I'm doing here. He smiles, and in a stunningly savvy moment, lets me hear a pointed observation, if not interpretation, that is exactly right: "You're letting Baldwin carry the heavy water, then you follow him."

I sit still, fail to suppress a smile, nod once again. Geoff nods, as well, at which point I feel irritated—just as, sometimes, my psychoanalytic supervisors got on my nerves when they said something to me about the patients I was learning to treat, under their watchful direction. I convert annoyance into an attempt at reconciling humor—say that a Latin School student gets an education outside of school as well as inside, and he readily agrees. We both, however, are wary of singling ourselves out, wary of feeling self-pity, with its implication of self-congratulation. Indeed, Geoff mocks us this way: "Poor you and me—all we have had to endure because we have attended that big-shot place." When you've been charged with doing something "wrong," for (in effect) becoming someone "uppity" and worse, you make the accusations of others enough your own (or so it can happen) that you're all too inclined to be under their spell, one way or another.

We did, eventually (not that day) talk a good deal about the "hazards," as it were, of leaving *any* neighborhood in Boston to attend a school that, by definition, singles out those who attend it: they have to be able students, and willing to take a demanding academic course of study that without exception leads toward college, even graduate school. As my young friend kept reminding me, his teachers will assume that their students will become doctors, lawyers, scientists, architects, scholars—pursue, almost all of them, advanced degrees. "It's an honor to be there," he adds, and then the "downside," he calls it: "If you try to reach high, lots of people will be left behind, and they won't like that and you'll know it." Then a question to me: "Should there be a Latin School—I mean, wouldn't it be easier if we were scattered in the local high schools of the city?" I think of what to say, but he quickly answers his own question with a thought that has also just crossed my mind: "Look, it'd be the same problem, I know, I'm sure of it: in the Jeremiah Burke School, or in South Boston High, or any other place [local high school] there would be tension between 'the college kids,' that's what we'd be called, and 'the rest of us,' that's what 'they' would call themselves. There's no getting away from it—what happens when you make your choice when you come to a fork in the road."

Thereupon, Geoff shifts our discussion, or apparently does; now he wants to talk about how hard it had been for him to *want* to play tennis, to *get* to play tennis, to *become* a (fairly good) tennis player. I keep nodding, and we both acknowledge that sports, like schools, can carry a lot of social baggage. I am moved mightily, listening to him talk about Arthur Ashe, his hero. He lets me know that he has a picture of Ashe on a small cork bulletin board his mom gave him—it hangs near his desk. Also on that bulletin board, a postcard picture of Julius Caesar that he discovered in a downtown Boston bookstore devoted to "classical" reading matter. He loves the juxtaposition, makes much of it—two conquerors, two individuals who dared cross rivers, explore and take control of new territory. I am not as impressed with Julius Caesar as I am with Arthur Ashe, but I remember through the fog of so many years how uncritically we all got swept up as we translated Caesar and Cicero—I guess I wanted this wonderfully knowing, astute youth to manage the irony he had summoned for Cicero in connection with Caesar, but that is me, now, I remind myself. Back then, we all were plugging for Caesar—none of us was asked to wonder who this person was, what he was trying to do, and why. Our job was to get him right by getting his words right: the narrowness of accomplishing careful translation, with no accompanying effort at historical analysis, interpretation. I wonder whether things have changed, and learn this quite unexpectedly: "Our Latin teacher pointed out to us that Caesar was a tough military leader, and he

was out there to expand the Roman empire, and we should realize that, and keep it in mind as we read him. But you're working half the night to get his sentences right, so you fall in line—you become a *miles,* one of his obedient soldiers!" Now I can laugh—we're both perched high on irony's mountain—though, again, as we seem to be learning during our extended talks, such an elevation can be morally dangerous: the ever-present temptation of smugness, self-congratulation.

In a sense, with a contemporary Latin School student's help, I was being pushed to a moral examination of excellence as it is institutionalized in a school's life, and as it gets pursued by hundreds of students each year in their everyday lives. I wondered how to pursue our conversation further. I had memories of reading Caesar, fully connecting with his military intentions, and that was that—until my dad pointed out to me that Rome was an *empire,* hence land-hungry for its own reasons of power and money. I also remember arguing with my dad, saying that Rome was threatened by various "tribes" (rather than people!)—and so had to take up arms against them. My dad, in turn, told me of his adolescence in England, when he read daily of lives lost by the hundreds, the thousands, in a war (on all sides) of greed and the fear it generated (the First World War). Fortunately for him, he became eligible to fight in that war only when it was over, though he lost a brother in it (the battle of Ypres with its mass slaughter). But I had no desire to be skeptical about Caesar and his Roman legions—and I certainly argued with my dad that it's hard to know about ancient wars what we can ascertain today about a recent confrontation. Yes, he agreed; but he pushed me, wondered what an ordinary fighting man of 1916 or 1917 would say in retrospect about trench warfare in France, as opposed to one of the generals who commanded the troops who massacred one another there. Surprised by such a bold conjecture, I retreated to my responsibilities: I had *my* do-or-die obligations, to study Caesar, to take his work to heart, to do well as an advocate of his, so I thought myself to be. I was the one who, after all, tried to figure out what the great leader had said, what he had done, and then spoke out loud (those graded "recitations"): a truth discovered, Caesar's as relayed to others through my hard work become my voice uttered in a still classroom.

Needless to say, I didn't put the matter that precisely, but my father most certainly got the message—I recall his face's recognition that a youth was standing up for old Julius Caesar out of an eager student's need to get through tough assignments with as much accommodating competence as he could summon: "ours not to reason why, ours but to do and die!" Dad apologized for "distracting" me, characterized himself, worriedly, as an "over-eager history buff." But as I went back to working out the meaning of Caesar's sentences, one after the other, I hearkened back to what had just happened between my father and me—I think I sensed that he had bowed to realpolitik: the need to let his son do well at all costs in school. If a certain "truth" be the victim, if a kind of historical curiosity and moral analysis be forsaken, then so be it: first things first!

There I was, decades later, now very much my father's son, trying to get a BLS student to have some second thoughts about Caesar—but this "lad" (as my English-born father called me, and would have called the youth with whom I was talking) would prove to be far more resourceful and plucky than I had ever been under such circumstances. All I had to do was ask him what he thought Arthur Ashe would think of Julius Caesar, if the two were ever to meet—and I got, as the saying goes, an earful: "That would be a scene! I'd want to have one of your tape recorders there, and a camera. I suspect Ashe would push Caesar hard—tell him off, maybe. I think of Ashe as really tough on the court, a fighter, as combative as they make them, but off-court, he was a real, true gentleman: quiet, friendly, never stooping to anger—but he made his point, I'll bet. He'd take old Julius aside, and he'd say, 'You were a great general, I hear. I never read your book, because I didn't take Latin. I had enough trouble trying to get on top

of my tennis game! But I've heard about all the battles you won, and that's great. We all fight in different ways! I worry about your men—that's my big problem, Julius: when your winning means lots of people losing their lives, that puts a big challenge to you. Whoever your God is, He'll want to have it out with you—why, why did you do this, and could you have done it without going to war?' That kind of question! I'm sure Julius would know what to say— hey, how many generals can write books! He's a good talker—that's why we read him. But God might join in, and push him a lot. Arthur would defer to God, but would Julius? It would be tense, that's what I think, big-time tense!"

As I hear this, I can't for the life of me understand why a youth who so readily imagines, constructs, a penetrating, indeed searing, exchange would want to have two such individuals so close to one another in his bedroom. I have the permission, hence the courage, to ask aloud about this pair—the reason for their life together, so to speak. I put my inquiry this way: "After hearing what you just said, I wonder why you have these two there in front of you all the time?" He immediately smiles, then tells me that I'm "too serious," that I've been "missing something." I don't have to ask him what—he sees the "what?" on my face and obliges my thirst for knowledge with a long outpouring, which I here condense: "It's an accident, first of all. I'll always have Ashe before me: he's my hero. I'll never be like him, up to him, but I've had enough experiences to make me think I've been tested like he was—I'm like him, a 'colored guy' who plays tennis (that's what my daddy's bossman used to call him; he'd say to his partner in the gas station, 'Hey, get that colored guy to come help me'). But this dude Caesar—hey, man, I just stumbled into him. He's my bossman for the day! [I look perplexed, so he explains.] He is lording it over all of us in my Latin class: 'OK, you guys, it's me calling the tune, and you picking up the beat! If you don't, you flunk—and not only this course: I could have your passport to college!' So, I go along to get along. My daddy said his daddy used to say that:

put him on a new medicine. Daddy said he'll never again just assume he can speak; he'll try to think about what he wants to say, and he'll thank the Lord for letting him stay here, and letting him be able to talk. The other day, he told me I should be grateful because I'm a black man, and I'm at that really 'big school' [his father's way of referring to Boston Latin], but I should watch my step there, and only open my mouth when I have something to say and I've made sure I know what I'm going to say. He told me something else, too; he told me that I should keep my ears open and my eyes. I should listen to what people are saying, and I should give them the 'once-over,' and try to get it straight in my mind *why* they're saying what they're saying—that's almost as important, sometimes as hearing them talk and understanding their message.

"I'm not saying I signed up with Daddy right away, on the dotted line. But he told me about some of his teachers (he never finished high school)—the good ones and the bad ones. He helped me see that you don't just surrender to someone, just because they've got a hold on you. For a long time he's told us kids to respect him and Mom (and other folks), but to speak up, when we think it's important, even if we end up disagreeing with him or with them. It's not easy to obey him on that score—that's where I become the rebel: I listen to him and I say yes, yes. Sometimes, he'll say, no, no, learn to say no as well as yes!

"My daddy educated himself. He goes to the library and reads. He tries to read up on a subject, and get all the sides he can. He says you're in trouble when you agree with people, and you don't look for any disagreement, because you want to be on the right side, and you've decided *this* is the right side, so that's the end of your thinking. It should be the *start* of your thinking—you should try to learn as much as you can. Daddy will take out these books, and he'll show me that one writer says A, and another B—and down the alphabet you go. I think of Daddy when I'm in Latin School. He sure wishes he could have gone there—but he came up hard, and his daddy

died young, and his mom, too, and he was brought up by an aunt, and she was tough, and then he learned to be an electrician, but because he was a black man, he had to be a 'helper,' and not a licensed man; that's how it was. People forget how it was! People forget a lot of things! That's what I'd like to tell the teachers, some of them—that they had slaves in Rome and in Greece, just like they did here, and we should be studying *that,* and for a few weeks, and we should be trying to think of what a slave could tell us about Rome, not just Cicero, and people like him. I'm not saying we don't need to read Cicero—sure we do. But we could remind ourselves every once in a while who this guy was, and we could realize there are some things he doesn't tell us anything about, so he's not as holy, holy as you might think. When he says, *asks: 'quam rem publicam habemus?'* and *'in qua urbe vivimus?'* then we should try to *answer* the man, not just let it be what the teacher calls a 'rhetorical question.' Do you see where I'm going?"

At last, yes, I was beginning to have some sense of his direction, his reasons for such a journey. The more he talked of his dad, whom I'd met only briefly, once or twice (he was always working, it seemed, often at night as well as during the day, to bring in money to his family, to save money for his son's college education), the more I connected him to Jude Fawley of Hardy's *Jude the Obscure:* Jude, the English yeoman of high aspirations; Jude, the autodidact who yearned for a Christminster (Oxford) education, yet was rebuffed because of his family background— and who, in one of the great scenes of the nineteenth-century English literary tradition (wherein Dickens, Eliot, and Hardy, especially, harnessed storytelling to social knowledge, moral introspection), took on the arrogance that can, not rarely, be found in old, distinguished educational institutions. Indeed, I would go back to Hardy's Jude after the above-described discussion with this Latin School student, and would eventually recommend that he read that novel. Jude's realization that there are hazards that come with the achievement of success, that people with great privileges and authority can become all too full of themselves and blind to all sorts of truths (and the people who know them) echoed in my mind when I did, finally, get to spend a couple of hours with the "Daddy" this youth kept mentioning—and how poignant it was to hear this hardworking, well-spoken, wonderfully thoughtful working man dream of entering the doors of the Latin School (he'd never done so), and drawing in its air, surely saturated in some mystical way (he sardonically said to me) with "Latin and Greek molecules that take your breath away!"

When for a moment I thought I detected some underlying seriousness in such expressed fancy, some soft spot of mistaken awe or even gullibility, some credulous acceptance of a vainglorious myth that he himself so often debunked (hence his son's skepticism, in this case an unacknowledged kind of humility, quite worthy of Jude's), I hastened to make clear how fit and just it was for all of us to worry about people and places, schools and colleges, regarded as 'the best,' as 'tops'—to which he nodded, but now wanted to add this: "I tell my son, I'll take my hat off to him or to some of his friends or his teachers, if they keep doing their learning together. That's what the school is for, and more power to them for all being smart—I just hope it doesn't go to their heads, that they're smart! The funny thing is, if that does happen—well, it's not so smart of them to let it happen! 'When you start learning things,' my momma used to tell me when I was a little wise guy, 'that's good, but don't let it go to your head, because you'll fall down real bad—you'll get tipsy on yourself, and a bad swollen head will hurt you a lot.' That's what she said, and here I am repeating it—a parent has to give his children any good advice he got growing up himself, it's his job."

Several weeks later his son would joke with me, wonder whether, somehow, his dad's words might be engraved on one of the walls of the Public Latin School, a bit of advice for class after class that enters, stays in order to be educated, leaves for "higher" learning. His rationale: "You know one of my teachers tells us that there's a big difference between

knowledge and wisdom, and every time he says that, I think of Daddy, and what he told you, and what I've heard from him over and over, as far back as I can recall him taking me aside and telling me something important from his heart. Maybe someone could translate his words into Latin! Maybe they could put his name after them [the words]—oh, he wouldn't mind 'anonymous.' Come to think of it, 'anonymous' would be best! It's what my dad calls 'hand-me-down advice' that's been passed and passed in our family! Think of it: we'd be walking down the corridor, and there'd be this anonymous message telling us to watch out, or we'll get into big trouble by getting all stuck on ourselves. Maybe no one would notice—like a fire in some closet, and you're too busy to notice, just hurrying along, but it could take you down, the whole house will burn, because you'll only try to do something when it's too late!

"I know it's a crazy idea I've had [he has reconsidered!]—why should I think they'd want to take my daddy's words and put them in this building? There are probably lots of mommas and daddies out there, whose kids are going to BLS, and they've given them plenty of good advice, and that doesn't mean you should go carving it into the school's walls, or translating it into Latin! I think my idea—well, I'm doing what Daddy warns me that I shouldn't do: I'm getting myself a big, big head over what he says. That's a good one! Like he says when he takes us in the car, 'Watch out'—around any corner some trouble can come at you: a driver who's drunk; a police car speeding so fast it heads slam-bang for you; someone crossing the street and not looking—there are dozens of dangers, and they can fall on you when you least expect them, so all you can do is keep yourself awake while you're at the wheel."

He jokes around, pretends he himself is at the wheel, uses his eyes and head to indicate the kind of alertness a careful driver has to mobilize. He acknowledges for the first time the moral watchfulness of some of his teachers—gives instances in which they have taken on directly the matter his father addresses in his brief homily: "There will be moments when a teacher stops us and reminds us that the big thing is how we 'behave'—with each other. 'I digress,' she'd say [he has been describing one such 'moment' in a favorite teacher's class, and he savors her choice of words], and then she'd let us know that she's grading us in her head for something else than those Latin vocabulary lists she hands out! She'd try to throw in some words about how we should respect each other, and it's funny, I remember that, what she said, better than the vocabulary words we were to memorize, or the reading we were translating."

I sit one morning (in 1997) in a classroom of a teacher whose praises he and others have sung long and loud and clear. Mrs. Wight is a most conscientious and articulate instructor of Latin and Greek. Her students range from seventh graders just starting to learn *amo, amas, amat* to seniors who have learned enough Greek to tackle Homer, no less, not to mention the intricacies of that extraordinarily subtle language, its tenses and moods, its modes of narrative expression a constant challenge, but, in the end, a source of pleasurable triumph for all those who persevere. This is not the Greek lesson I remember. The passage being read is the same, but a different notion obtains of what the study of Greek literature ought entail. The boys and girls, of all sorts and conditions (as the expression in the Book of Common Prayer describes it), sit casually, yet with obvious seriousness as the teacher makes connections between a Greek text and other words, to be found in writers of English and Latin; moreover, we are asked to look at maps, to study vases, to reflect upon historical matters as they shape the imagination of those who tell stories that over the centuries become emblematic in nature: a legend of continual significance across the oceans of time and space.

In the midst of this I realize how variously, mischievously, pride asserts itself, how quickly we can be engulfed by what George Eliot called "unreflecting egoism." Out of nowhere, it seems, I find myself feeling disgruntled, cranky, ostensibly worried about these young men and women. They aren't moving

at a fast enough clip, I decide, in their classroom translation. They are being distracted (I go further) by talk of artifacts in museums or archaeological digs, by references to "sagas" written in other languages. I can hear my old, crusty, demanding, and ever so knowing and able Greek teacher, Henry Rozalvin Gardner (a prize named after him now goes to a student who does well at Greek), telling us to "keep moving along," as he said again and again, followed by a slogan that I've never forgotten: "a page a day," meaning our decided obligation to do a hefty amount of translation out loud during each class, no matter what. *He* wouldn't tolerate these "diversions," I hear myself calling a teacher's concerted effort to bring a Greek class alive, draw lines from it to other fields of inquiry and reflection. Moreover, these students seem so *relaxed*—what *is* it with them, with their teacher? Why no apparent anxiety as the clock ticks? Where are the surprise vocabulary tests, sprung on us with no forewarning, in the midst of a spell of translation? Why wasn't the teacher *grading* the students publicly, thereby keeping everyone on his or her toes? How about some daily exercises in memorization with recitations meant to prove that we not only knew how to make our way, as the expression went, "from Greek to English," but we were willing and able (indeed, eager) to engrave huge swaths of Xenophon or Homer in our minds, never to be forgotten, or so we thought then, and surprisingly, to a considerable degree, so we have discovered the case to be?

Such questions, of course, had to be answered by me alone, and so doing, I tried in vain to remember the advice my young informant's father had offered—I was, alas, quite attracted, then and there, to the notion that in the proverbial "old days," we (I) had gotten a far better education than is now available at this school, and maybe, any school. It took a few minutes for the implication of this nostalgia to dawn upon me: I was witness to the unfolding of a rather stirring and effective kind of broadly classical education, and so the more I realized how lucky its recipients were, the more I recognized my own relative ill luck—and soon enough, as a consequence, a rally to my defense, an effort of the mind to justify its own experience when presented with (threatened by) the sight and sound of quite another experience, one that in my own teaching in schools and in a college I would ordinarily try to remember carefully, in order to emulate. It must have been too much, unfortunately, for me to observe a group of students having a reasonably relaxed time as they worked hard, indeed, to learn what a most talented and skillful teacher was imparting to them with imagination and verve. Had I only been less wrapped in my own memories, and the excuses they demand we make for them, I might have embraced more quickly what was so evidently impressive and affecting about this class. In the end, however, the tide turned, to the point that I kept thinking of Mrs. Wight as Mrs. Wright, much to the amusement of several of her students, who were glad to tell me that she most certainly was Mrs. Right—so they had heard before they "got" her, and so they have learned to believe during this school year.

On the way home that day I kept thinking of W. Somerset Maugham's *Of Human Bondage,* but with no idea why. When I got home, I went to my desk and tried to sort out some books and correspondence haphazardly placed in several stacks. Then I took the books back to their proper places on nearby shelves. Then I noticed (one of those accidents or incidents we have learned in this century to take seriously) an old volume of that novel of Maugham's—my dad's copy, which I can remember him reading a second time while I was, yes, a student at the Public Latin School. (He and my mom read to one another several times a week, so my brother and I could hardly *not* know what stories they were attending.) But I had no notion, still, why that novel should attract my attention, nor did I immediately pick it out, try to find out the reason, or better, my reasons. Only later that day did I return to that bookshelf, in order to look at Maugham's novel. By then I knew that something inside me was "at work" (the psychoanalyst I saw for many years often used that plain phrase to more

than hint at evidence of unconscious activity). I even had my train of thought figured: that novel tells of a boy's, a young man's, personal journey—his relationship with a range of individuals. Surely these Latin School youths, so obviously on their own particular voyage, if not pilgrimage, had inspired me to remember Maugham's version of "growing up," of "finding oneself."

In any event, I browsed and for moments settled into certain pages, even a whole chapter or two. I didn't seem, however, to be making any great discovery about a specific connection between that novel and anything I'd recently seen or done, and, actually, had lost all (conscious) interest in doing so—but then, as I perused my dad's notes, scribbled inside the first (empty) pages of the book, I noticed a phrase of his, with one word lightly underlined: "an *old* school," and then another phrase, "dead languages." In no time I was reading this: "The King's School at Tercanbury, to which Philip went when he was thirteen, prided itself on its antiquity"; and this: "The masters had no patience with modern ideas of education, which they read of sometimes in *The Times* or *The Guardian,* and hoped fervently that King's School would remain true to its old traditions. The dead languages were taught with such thoroughness that an old boy seldom thought of Homer or Vergil in after life without a qualm of boredom; and though in the common room at dinner one or two bolder spirits suggested that mathematics was of increasing importance, the general feeling was that they were a less noble study than the classics. Neither German nor chemistry was taught, and French only by the form masters; they could keep order better than a foreigner, and since they knew the grammar as well as any Frenchman, it seemed unimportant that none of them could have got a cup of coffee in the restaurant at Boulogne unless the waiter had known a little English."

With these words I put the book down, and gazed out the window to my right. Before me was the usual scene of some grass, and then a line of fairly tall trees, but I wasn't really paying any of that the slightest heed; rather, I was looking across years, decades, to a school not exactly like the King's School, but in certain respects not unlike it, either. No question, ideologically, the similarity was there—we learned how to read French, for instance, but not speak it; and always, we learned that Latin and Greek were the most important subjects, with English literature falling well behind them, but ahead, in rank, of chemistry or physics, for sure: a lean, tough, classical curriculum, taught by, again, "masters," *some* of whom might have been welcomed by Maugham's King's School. It was possible for me, courtesy of that novel, to get some distance on my past, and, very important, on what I'd just that very day experienced. An author sent his fictional character to a crusty, self-important school, where one got a "good education," in preparation for one of "the four professions to which it was possible for a gentleman to belong." Maugham's school, though, is in transition—a new headmaster is bent on shaking it up, a mighty task. So it has been with Latin School's history, or that of other long-lived institutions, including the nation's oldest college, across the Charles from its predecessor of one year in Boston. Indeed, when William James taught at Harvard, at the height of his success, in the 1890s, he wrote stinging letters of disapproval, even disdain—a felt scorn with respect to the institutional rigidities, the moral complaisance, and, not least, the decided *hauteur* that he couldn't help noticing and taking to heart as an insider who had an uncanny ability, at the same time, to be a critical outsider. I thought of him, too, that evening—in a way, he and Maugham helped me to understand an African-American father (and, surely, hundreds of other parents like him) who had yet to enter a building, yet knew so very much about it, and who admired what it represented while at the same time worrying about its flaws, even as Maugham tried to evoke the distinctive accomplishments of a school that was also in great need of reform—and likewise James, ever the trenchant and voluble and daring observer, but also an unrelenting judge.

In a recent visit to the Latin School I asked one of the students if she'd ever been to the nearby Museum of Fine Arts, or the Gardner Museum, almost directly across the street from the backyard of the school. She was astonished at the question— why, *of course* she'd been to both places, many times. I then wondered whether such visits had anything to do with her academic work, and again, with a certain perplexity (this fellow has a penchant for weird questions!): *of course* she (and her classmates) valued those museums as "treasure-house places," where students can continue to expand upon what they have studied in various classes. The more we talked about museums, the more I realized that not only a school's curriculum has changed in recent years. To draw on W. H. Auden's phrase, used in his memorial poem to Freud, the Latin School has tried to live up to its linguistic tradition, but integrate into it the social and cultural world of late-twentieth-century American urban life, hence "a whole climate of opinion" that has broken with a past of notable, proudly embraced insularity: a privileged, college-bound few who had no need of immersing themselves in the contemporary affairs of a particular era's city (or state, or nation). To be sure, in the past some of the school's students, once grown-up citizens, had more than acquitted themselves in that regard, as citizens, as a reading of their names, inscribed in the auditorium, most certainly attests. But for generations the school had been self-consciously aloof—had placed little emphasis on contemporary events, struggles. Rather, we were told and told, the Latin School was first, *there* before all others, *there* at the very start of America's European settlement, and so the phrase "old school ties" had a literal as well as educational or social or ideological significance: an institution whose life has been synonymous with that of our nation's history, as well as a *Latin* school, hence the repository of a long academic tradition until recently pursued in colleges as well as high schools or preparatory schools. (In the nineteenth century Latin and Greek were not what they now are at Harvard, a field of concentration for a relative handful, but rather an utterly essential part of a university experience.)

Somewhat neglected in years past was an emphasis on the first word, the *Public* Latin School. No question, the school *was* public, in the sense that its students were day students, and entitled to an education as a right, rather than as a consequence of payment. Still, there were "standards": both those asked of the aspirants or candidates (not all children, by any means, sought to attend the school) and those required of the teachers and administrators, who chose the young people who would be accepted and certified them as graduates, thereby affirming to the world something about the presumed intellectual competence or performance of youths before they'd even stepped in a classroom, and too, of course, after they'd finished their last class. The moral hazards of such a means of selection, such a commitment of instruction, are not hard to figure— a smugness, a self-importance, a self-congratulation that become hard to challenge because they are not, alas, challenged from within, as it were: made the stuff of constant, collective worry, of a concern that is acknowledged and discussed, as in the worry on the part of the Hebrew prophets and of Jesus of Nazareth that pride (that sin of sins) lurks around many corners, hence the observation (Matthew) that "the last shall be first, the first last," not exactly a remonstrance meant to reassure the ever so accomplished graduates of either Boston Latin School or its almost equally old Cambridge "friend," Harvard College. I *do,* however, recall one uneasy moment in my Latin School stay that oddly prefigures this discussion (and what has prompted it, a school's transformation).

Only in the early 1960s would the Supreme Court forbid a resort to the Holy Scriptures in the nation's public schools; and so, often in the morning our "homeroom" teachers at Latin School would read from the Old Testament or the New Testament—especially common were sections from Isaiah and Jeremiah, from Ecclesiastes, from the gospel of Matthew, from Paul's letters to the

Corinthians, Romans. Not that (unfortunately) any effort was made to tell us about the way the history of ancient Greece and Rome connected to the history of the Jews of that time, including one of their people whom others, versed in Latin or Greek, would come to worship. Rather, the teachers would simply read, and hope we ourselves did the work of getting the (moral) point; or else, they followed the reading with a brief comment or two in order that we would all be given a moment or longer of pause. How well, then, I remember the time Charles Ward French (he with the shock of white hair, and the stern Yankee visage, which included rimless glasses through which he peered relentlessly and judged sternly) read from Matthew about this world's first and last, their respective destinies in a future (otherworldly) scheme of things—and then the hush in the class, a tribute to the intensity he supplied his reading, as if he was thereby saying: for God's sake (literally!) pay these words close heed, for they are utterly revolutionary in nature; they aim to turn things upside down—in Nietzsche's phrase, which you might soon (we were seniors) meet in a college philosophy course, they are words meant to herald a "transvaluation of values." Yet, Master French wouldn't settle for the tautly suggestive reading itself, or the serious mien of his that he made a point of demonstrating, or the pointed silence that he (often quite voluble) now presented to us. Rather, he suddenly erupted: "Not words without significance for us here, now."

No more said—a wry, cryptic remark with two negatives, and an insistence that what got spoken be carried across space and time, linked to our school, our contemporary lives. I can still hear his silence become ours—a puzzled class confounded. Why those biblical words? Why has this old Yankee, a stern, hardy soul in his sixties, seen fit to saddle us with this riddle, this declaration of the topsy turvy? To bring us to our knees; to bring us to our senses; to throw some monkey wrench into our spirited, confident lives, then on the virtual brink of a new spurt of success (those college acceptance letters, in all their glory become ours, around the next corner)? What did he *mean?*—we asked, we who knew Greek and Latin and French and now were having ostensible trouble with the King's English (specifically that of King James). Soon enough, the summons of our own version of psychology, at a time when, to repeat, that discipline had yet to become a crucial element in a nation's regular thinking: he must be getting "old"; he has always been a cranky one, but today he is stretching things mightily—oh, well, soon we'll all be elsewhere (on our way to being, ever more, the first, or, as we'd learned to think of ourselves, say of ourselves, οἱ Ἕλληνες, rather than οἱ πολλοί).

These days, in contrast, that word "public" has returned in glory to the school to whose name it belongs. These days, for the far better rather than for the worse, the old school is part of a Boston world, an American world of "all sorts and conditions," a building with past treasures to its name, but today's serious demands to consider—the desire of "the many," as never before, to join those Greek cadres, to share their authority of mind and soul, to wear their badges of honor, to partake of their privileges, and, yes, to experience at last the vulnerabilities that go with success, with being "the first," rather than those known ever so long among "the last." No wonder, then, in that Greek class in the Public Latin School on a May morning an African-American young woman glided through a lesson with obvious diligence, with an excellence learned through diligence—and in a relaxed moment made knowing reference to Shakespeare's *Antony and Cleopatra,* to the "triumvirs" Antony, Caesar, and Lepidus, to the friends of Antony, of Caesar, of Pompey, to Octavia, Caesar's sister, Antony's wife, to Cleopatra and her two "attendants," whose names the student knew, Charmian and Iras. As I learned of her learning, I learned, too, of what I was never asked to learn, and I knew in an instant that even if I had been asked to do so "back then," the chances would have been low that I'd have kept in mind the names of Cleopatra's attendants—even as they never commanded any of my attention when I did encounter them in Cambridge. But this was Boston, and even as Rosencrantz and Guildenstern had evoked the attention of us in a mid-twentieth-century Public Latin School, Charmian and Iras were very much alive in this end-of-a-century, end-of-a-millennium classroom.

Perkins School for the Blind

Located in Watertown, Massachusetts, Perkins School for the Blind, chartered in 1829, was among the first such institutions in the United States. In addition to educating the blind and visually impaired, the Perkins School admits students with handicaps such as deafness and some degree of mental retardation. The following photographs were made in 1992. Comments accompanying the photographs are from interviews conducted by George Howe Colt.

When Joel came here he was considered autistic. He used to be alone, really by himself, an island. Now he has made connections to people. In music class he gets really, really excited, starts flailing and slapping, and then someone comes and puts a hand on his shoulder and it soothes him, reminds him, "I'm with other people."

The thing with Joel is he's starting to take control of his own life, not just letting himself be walked through it. He'll let you know what he likes, what he doesn't like, what he expects from you. We'll start toward the gym and he'll suddenly start singing, "I can see clearly now the rain has come," and he's saying, "It's time for music." When he suddenly wishes he was with someone, he'll say, "Oh, he misses Timmy." When he doesn't want to do something he'll say, "Mad at Perkins."

Joel Geiger, 19, Secondary Services Program, described by his teacher

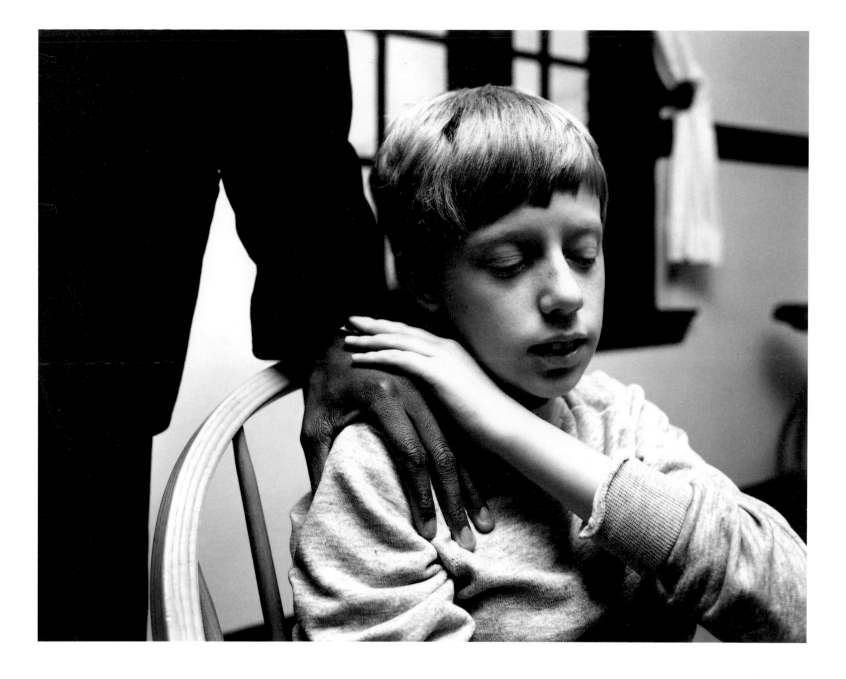

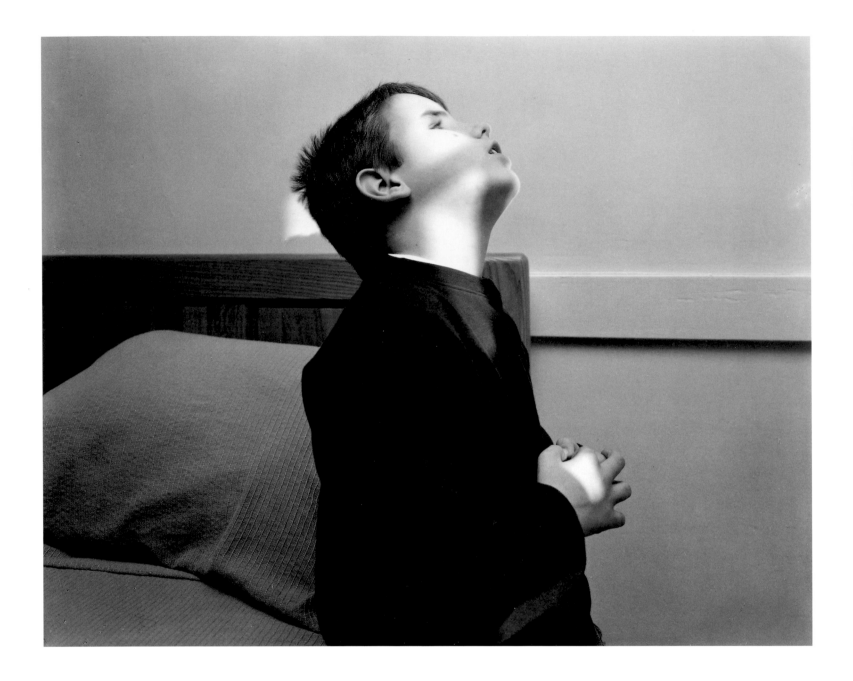

I love going for long walks. I'm definitely thinking about being a physical therapist. I want to be able to help people walk that can't walk well, because I feel bad that they have to miss out on a lot of things. They can't run races, ride bikes, swim, or take long walks, especially people that are paralyzed. When I first came to Perkins I was scared because I didn't know whether I would make any friends. But I quickly felt very happy. At my old school, they used to make fun of me, like on the bus. It was good to be in a school where people didn't make fun of me. I like TV, but I love the radio more because you don't have to see it. I used to like oldies, but now I like country music best. I used to pretend I was a radio station announcer, but I couldn't do that in public school, because everyone would think I was weird or funny. At Perkins, people wouldn't think it was weird.

Sarah Male, 14, Lower School Program

Signs: "I like the moon. I like the planets. My favorite planet is Earth."

Heather loves planets and the solar system, and learning about astronauts. She'll sign rocket. She wanted to know all the signs for astronaut, rocket, space, planets, wind, weather. One night, when we were walking back from gym to cottage, she pointed at the moon, and signed moon; later, when we found the moon in one of her books, she understood that the moon in the sky was the same one as she saw in her books, that there were planets surrounding it, and she was so thrilled, she wanted to learn all about space. Now, every time we go outside at night, she points out the moon and makes the sign for moon.

Heather Smith, 13, Deaf-Blind Program, described by her teacher

Before, Ian wouldn't let you touch him. Now he understands that it's a way of communicating. Now he likes physical contact, enjoys hugs, likes to dance. This year he's exploring the other students—touching them gently. He is understanding that there are other people in his world. He's into smell; he will smell hair, hands, to recognize someone. And he's beginning to understand signs. Last year he could mimic signs. This year he can sign eat, drink, more, and bed. That's very exciting.

Ian Levasseur, 16, Deaf-Blind Program, described by his teacher

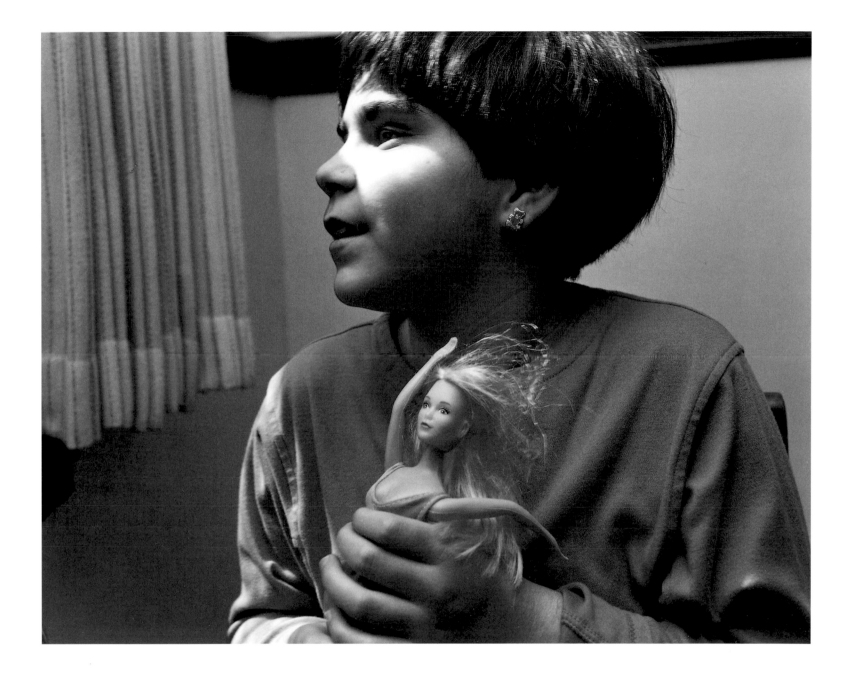

Kerri loves the light. When she walks into a room, she'll get in front of a window, and stay there in the light. If she passes a window, she'll turn toward it. She'll get stuck on light, and might stay there until someone gives her a tap. She likes to move her hand up and down in front of her face to play with the light, perhaps because it's one of the few things she can recognize and control. She has a favorite spot in every room, depending on where the light is; she is always moving toward the light.

Kerri McNulty, 15, Deaf-Blind Program, described by her teacher

You know how in the spring you see the yellow in the grass? Not the daffodils, not the buttercups. The dandelions. I like to smell them and then I get powder up my nose. You can find a lot beside the playground. I used to pick them a lot. They are my favorite. Put them up to your nose and you get powder on your nose. Flower powder. One day, after they mowed the grass, there was only one dandelion left, and I was happy, I took it home, and put it in some water until it died. I can't wait for spring so I can pick those again.

Jessica Flores, 11, Lower School Program

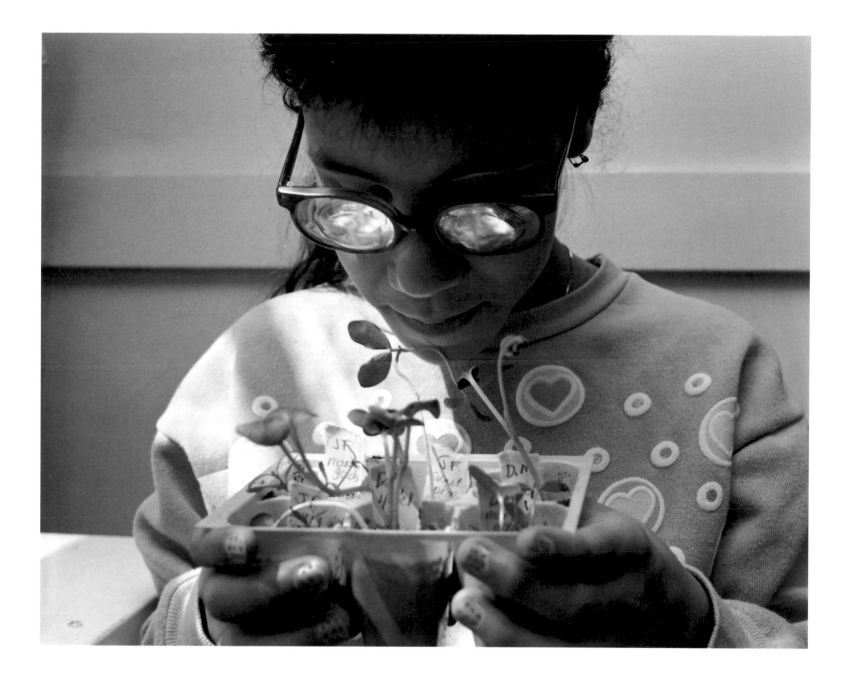

This is my fourth year at Perkins. At my old school people were mean. They criticized and made fun of me and asked me why I look a different way. But I don't look much different from anyone else. I was happy to get here. There's not as much pressure. People don't criticize. They don't walk around me and bother me. I can sit and be peaceful. . . . But it's my last year and I'm looking forward to leaving. I'm ready for a job. I might work in a secretarial school so I can be a typist. Or maybe work in a flower store, helping arrange flowers. Or maybe work in a clothing store, hanging clothes on a rack—especially colorful clothes. My vision is pretty bad, but I can see colors.

Astlene Nelson, 21, Secondary Services Program

Truth Comes in Degrees

One of our teachers at Boston Latin School often rose to the occasion of any evident (or even implied) self-pity with a vigorous reminder to us of our good fortune, whatever our social or economic circumstances. We were, by and large, healthy, he kept on pointing out, no matter any health problems we might have had. We could walk and run, talk and listen, look and see—whereas he had a brother who was born virtually sightless, and by the time he was of school age (five or six) was declared "legally blind." He had never clearly seen his mother or his father, or our (Latin) teacher—had never clearly seen himself. Several times, most affectingly, we as self-conscious teenagers, ever so directly or slyly concerned with our appearance, were prompted to think of what we simply took for granted, the ease with which we might touch base with ourselves, check on ourselves, through a quick and eager, or reluctant resort to a mirror. I remember such moments because of a teacher's intensely felt subjectivity as it got communicated to us—but also because we each had personal reasons to receive an intended moral perspective in ways very much our own: we became sardonic, indeed—told one another that our sighted fate is one worse than blindness! Such a line of assertion was not meant to be callous or mean-spirited —only, in the tradition of egoism, self-pitying. After all, this teacher was one of our toughest; he demanded a full page of Vergil from us every day—a Latin-to-English translation, and a readiness to "take" (the verb he used!) a vocabulary or grammar test on what we'd read. He also gave us a daily string of nouns and verbs and adjectives and adverbs to memorize, to the point that we called him, sometimes, "Chalky" —the teacher who was ever ready to write lists and more lists, assignments and what he called his "second thoughts" (additional assignments) on the blackboard. So, we smiled ironically, mused to ourselves that we wouldn't mind at all being blind—that way we'd be spared the heaviest burden challenging us, taxing us, nightly. We knew, of course, that we didn't mean literally what we were saying—that, actually, the mere fact that we were imagining ourselves blind as a blessing of sorts indicated how effectively our teacher had gotten to us, given us some pause.

We heard more from that teacher once or twice—his story of his brother's educational story: he had been a student at Perkins School for the Blind, the oldest such school in America, even as we were ever prepared to remember our own school's age. We also heard from him about Charles Dickens's visit to that school and (again, our egoism!) we wanted to know whether he'd ever visited *our* school. No, we were told—whereupon we wondered what the great novelist's priorities were, why he would forsake "us" for "them"! In fact, Dickens the novelist, who was always sensitive to human vulnerability and pain, was keen (during his 1842 lecture tour of America) to visit places of such hurt, suffering, psychological or physical marginality—hence his visit not only to Perkins, but to a "State Hospital for the insane" in Boston. Once our teacher promised to obtain Dickens's *American Notes,* to read from that nonfiction of the great English nineteenth-century master; but he was loath to surrender any of his demanding time with us as we struggled so mightily with Vergil. More than a decade later, my wife, Jane, who for years taught English literature, including several of Charles Dickens's novels, would mention the "social writing" that he did when he visited America. Her family had been closely involved with the Perkins School for several generations—and her father, John Hallowell, was a member of the board of trustees of the institution when Jane and I got married. She had visited the school; and she once directed me to her favorite passages of Dickens with regard to his visit there, and, most especially, this paragraph: "It is strange to watch the focus of the blind, and see how free they are from all concealment of what is passing in their thoughts. Observing which, a man with eyes may blush to contemplate the mask he wears. Allowing for one shade of anxious expression which is never absent from their countenances, and the like of which we may readily detect in our own focus if we try to feel our way in the dark, every idea, as it rises within them, is expressed with the lightning's speed and nature's truth. If the company at a rout, or drawing-room at court, could only for a time be as unconscious of the eyes upon them as blind men and women are, what secrets would come out, and what a worker of hypocrisy this sight, the loss of which we so much pity, would appear to be!"

There he is, the storyteller as knowing and subtle psychological observer, taking direct aim not only at the blind, but at the rest of us, for whom eyes serve to help us conceal, rather than bear witness. No wonder, then, Anna Freud, the founder, really, of the discipline of child psychoanalysis, once commented upon our use of the eyes and ears in this manner: "We take in the world through seeing it and hearing it—but then comes the censoring we do. There is

only so much we want to remember of what we have actually seen or heard, and so we often quickly forget some of what we've seen and heard firsthand. I will ask my analytic patients what they 'actually' saw or heard, and because I use that word [actually], I have put them on alert as to my intentions—and so, rather commonly they will tell me that they 'half-know' that they blot out certain 'things' they see or hear, certain people who have been 'there,' but are 'wiped out.' One of my patients put it this way to me: 'There's a lot I don't notice—in one ear out the other, as people say, and with the eyes, it's as if I'm partially blind: I miss what I don't want to see.' Now, he was a biologist, not a psychologist, and he wanted to spend a lot of time [in his analytic experience with Miss Freud] trying to understand what he kept calling 'the neurophysiology of the matter'—[by which] he meant the way in which his 'sensory organs,' he kept on calling them, either 'register' or don't register certain people or places or objects. I had to keep bringing him back to our purpose in that room— to figure out the emotional reasons for his 'partial vision,' or his 'partial hearing.' But after he would leave, I myself would reflect on what he was trying to figure out: how we can be blind or deaf, those of us whose eyes and ears are one hundred percent in working order!"

At that time I was working in the South, continuing studies I'd begun years earlier (in 1960) on school desegregation, its psychological consequences for black and white children. I remembered two blind children I'd met in Birmingham, Alabama, in 1964, and remembered the school to which they were sent. Alabama's Institute for the Deaf and the Blind was founded two years before the Civil War began. It is now a nationally known and respected institution located in Talladega, about fifty miles east of Birmingham. I remember Anna Freud mentioning AIDB, as it is known, during a discussion of the special challenges that fate puts to blind and deaf children as they grow up. She and her colleagues in child psychoanalysis were much interested in such children and had done some substantial work with them, especially blind boys and girls. Miss Freud asked about AIDB in the way foreigners often do when they come to a country with only a finite amount of knowledge about its geography. She came regularly to New Haven and New York, was no stranger to certain other cosmopolitan cities, but the South was not her regular beat. With a certain wistfulness she looked around the Yale dormitory room where we had been sitting and then made a comment I can still hear: "I'd like to go visit that school [AIDB] one day."

She never realized that wish, but she would certainly be enthralled by the results of someone else's visit. Frederick Wiseman's four film documentaries run nine hours: an effort to show how the blind, the deaf, or those blind and deaf (and impaired in other ways, too) manage at a residential school, and while there become reasonably educated, even begin to make their way in the outside world. With his films, Wiseman has been directing a school, of sorts, for three decades: he has wanted to help us overcome our own versions of blindness and deafness. He started his documentary career with the still controversial *Titicut Follies,* a film about a Massachusetts hospital for the criminally insane. (For a long time I couldn't show that film to my medical students without obtaining their signatures—a collective declaration that they are an educational audience rather than mere film buffs.) Some Massachusetts officials worried that the "privacy" of certain inmates was violated—though the utterly outrageous and degrading circumstances shown in the film seem to have troubled those officials rather less. To this day, the hospital earns consistently negative ratings, and is a recurrent subject of journalistic muckraking.

After he had completed *Titicut Follies*—despite his troubles with Bay State bureaucrats—Wiseman turned his attention to one institution after another: a high school, a court, a department store, a hospital, a racetrack, a seminary, a city's welfare system, a place where young military recruits are indoctrinated, a slaughterhouse that enables us to have meat on our tables. Each film is meant to place us who watch in the midst of a particular social and institutional scene, in the hope that as we view people going about their chores, doing what they are paid to do or required by law or custom to do, and hear what is said (or shouted or whispered), we will know rather more about our large and complex nation.

These four documentaries amount to Wiseman's most ambitious project yet. "Before I made these films my experience and knowledge of deaf and/or blind people was limited, practically nonexistent," Wiseman explained. "When I began to think about it I realized that I had never gone to school with anyone who was deaf or blind, nor did I have any contact in my work or social life with anyone who was without one or both of these basic senses." Of the four films, *Blind* and *Deaf* are the two basic texts. They aim to show how children make do without sight or hearing—learn to take care of themselves, to read and write, to get on successfully with others, to negotiate their way in a world where vision is taken for granted, as is the capacity to understand the spoken word. *Multi-Handicapped* and *Adjustment and Work* take us further along: to the more strenuous difficulties of those who are both deaf and deaf-mute (or have, for instance, cerebral palsy as an additional disability); and to the adulthood of those who have attended AIDB, and now hope to find work, achieve a significant degree of personal and financial independence.

Each of the four films invites us, first, to the South, to Talladega, Alabama: the country roads, the fields with their crops, the Winn Dixie market, the homes, modern and Victorian, the courthouse, and, inevitably, a strip, with its gas stations, honky-tonk stores, fast-food restaurants. All four present a Southern city's social life—the genteel white neighborhoods, the modest homes of working-class white or black families, the streets where impoverished blacks struggle for survival. All four also offer sights and sounds many of the children who attend AIDB have missed: the well-known Talladega stock-car racetrack, with its zooming machines and boisterous crowds, the predictably mock-elegant world of mall shopping, and, most affecting, the simple but powerful noise of the railroad engine—Willa Cather's "cold, vibrant scream."

Deaf and *Blind* essentially chronicle the way children in two quite unusual residential school settings spend their time. Early in *Blind,* we notice one form of affluence—the sunglasses of those who can afford to dim their vision. Minutes later we meet boys and girls who are learning to feel their way along corridors, who follow voices, who brave their own kind of adventures. The students are black and white, boy and girl, quite bright and average in intelligence and retarded. No matter, they hold hands, they seem thoroughly at ease with one another—blind in a different sense of the word to differences the rest of us are quick to regard as important, even when quite young.

Not able to notice skin color or the kind of clothes worn, they attend to the texture of cement or wood or glass—what it feels like when a cane (or one's hand) moves from one part of a building to another. They learn with the cane to sight an approaching door or set of stairs. They learn not so much to rely on the cane as to master it. With no embarrassment or sense of irony they and their teachers talk of going to "see" what is out there awaiting them—paths to trod, directions to pursue, choices to make. They "keep looking." They "watch for" landmarks. They listen hard. They find a water fountain and feel the obvious satisfactions of an important discovery.

They play sports. They learn Braille. They let their fingers feel the way to a control of a needle, some thread: knitting, sewing. They talk with their teachers about family troubles—a drunken father, a broken marriage, a disappointment experienced on a home visit. They feel low and hesitant at times. But they are constantly encouraged, complimented—in soft, Southern drawls that seem especially fitting for such occasions. Throughout the film the camera is kept constantly busy—moving from room to room, activity to activity: children playing, cooking, learning to make change, creating messes,

cleaning up after themselves, dancing, and, finally, getting ready for bed. As they pray before falling asleep—a particularly poignant moment—the film begins to conclude. The moon is out. The lights of the city are turned on. Soon, though, all will be darkness—though for these children there is, alas, no such transition.

Deaf (two hours, 43 minutes) is half an hour longer than *Blind.* The structure of *Deaf* is similar to that of *Blind*—the camera's constant attention to a school day's events. Children learn to sign, to read lips as well, and, not least, to use their vocal chords, to talk—no easy task for someone who has not heard himself or herself speak, never mind anyone else. Gradually Wiseman's camera informs us of the special technology a contemporary school for deaf children requires—lights for a phone or a clock-alarm, closed captioned television, a "minicom" typewriter that enables telephone conversation. But teachers matter more than those devices—what happens between them and their students as they try to comprehend each other. Some of the teachers are deaf themselves, and their earnest professional devotion obviously draws on reservoirs of personal experience.

The centerpiece of *Deaf* offers a family squabble (something by no means peculiar to AIDB children and their parents). A fourteen-year-old boy has threatened suicide several times, declared his mother indifferent to him. She has driven to the school from Mobile, and for three-quarters of an hour we watch her, her son, a wise and empathic counselor, and the school's principal talk about what is happening to a family. The biological father has spurned Peter because of his deafness, yet even though a stepfather likes him, pays him favorable attention, he yearns for his "first daddy." The estrangement between mother and son is obvious—the aloofness each uses for self-protection, the hurt pride each displays.

All over the world youths and parents struggle with one another in similar ways for similar reasons. What distinguishes this confrontation is the obvious difficulty a mother and a son have in speaking to each other. The mother's signing is inadequate, and the youth is ready at a glance to use such a failure as an indictment of her. Not that, of course, parents and children who have excellent hearing are spared such family impasses. Wiseman dwells on this scene not to show a special psychopathology, but to remind us of universals that transcend difficulties such as deafness—the failures of trust and love that mark the lives of so many of us.

In all four of Wiseman's documentaries, teachers are heard at some length discussing the progress of various students, their small victories and persisting troubles. Often the talk becomes psychological—the dreary jargon one hears everywhere in this country today. Several times the viewer is transported from a concrete, arresting teaching situation to an abstract psychological discussion, with banal words such as "individuation" and "adjustment" filling, if not fouling, the air. So it goes, the bemused filmmaker seems to be telling us.

At such moments I kept wishing Anna Freud *had* visited AIDB—or the Perkins School—before she died. She had little use for psychological pretentiousness, and enormous respect for the daily fortitude and intelligence of the many teachers she knew in the course of her life. She never patronized them with overblown psychoanalytic language. Often enough, I remember, she presented herself as the one who needed to learn—and she would have learned a lot had she gone to Alabama, or, for that matter, seen Wiseman's films. She put in a considerable number of clinical hours observing and working with blind children, and in volume five of her *Writings* ("Research at the Hampstead Child-Therapy Clinic and Other Papers") she several times takes note of the stumbling blocks and quandaries blindness and deafness (or bodily impairments of various kinds) can present to children. The young take in the world—including the image of a mother, a father, and, needless to say, themselves—through the use of the eyes: the sight of others, the sight of oneself in a mirror or a picture taken. The young also hear the words "yes" and "no" every day—the encouragement and the disapproval that go to make a conscience that works effectively (but not imperiously, crazily) in later life.

It is probably no accident that *Deaf* is a noisier film than *Blind,* and has more truculence in it. In the former the teachers at times—no matter the camera's presence—seem sorely tested, even on the verge of an outburst or two. The deaf children are more combative, the blind more self-effacing. In psychoanalytic language, the deaf sometimes experience special hurdles in "super-ego formation"; the blind may be particularly tested by the vicissitudes of "narcissism." For years, however, Anna Freud urged on her psychoanalytic colleagues restraint in such formulations, common sense in their application to individuals or groups of people, and, most insistently, the research initiative she called "direct observation"—with theoretical conjecture kept to a minimum until, as she once put it, "we have something to contemplate." Wiseman's films would have held her close attention, prompted her, I suspect, to want to look at the entire footage he secured in Talladega.

Even as the psychoanalyst must struggle with his or her subjectivity, a filmmaker such as Wiseman presents us with a mix of objective reportage and a particular artist's attitude. He is at pains to let us hear the school officials talk about budgets and political lobbying in the state capital, Montgomery, because he wants to make the point that lots of the sensitivity and compassion we have witnessed is enabled by tough, shrewd behind-the-scenes bargaining sessions. He asks us to listen to A.D. Gaston, the ninety-two-year-old black Birmingham entrepreneur, talking of "dream power," of *his* "handicapped" (segregated) earlier life as a grandson of slaves, born in turn-of-the-century poverty, because the speech is animated and entertaining, but also, one suspects, because yet another big shot comes across as occasionally full of himself and full of hot air, and we had best remember that neither blindness nor deafness (Gaston's words are translated beautifully into sign language) need deny anyone an exposure to life's funny or absurd moments. Wiseman the filmmaker and editor is Wiseman the visual poet, the social critic, the ironist—someone probing social reality, yes, but also arranging it, composing it, as artists or writers always do. During the days I watched these four powerful films, I kept reading reviews of them, and biographical accounts of the man who had to fight hard, against considerable odds, to make them, to have them shown uncut. He is on record as taking on the very people whose power can stand between his work and thousands of viewers, the Corporation for Public Broadcasting, where an endemic Anglophilia often threatens, and where, in Wiseman's words, "personal politics, the buddy system, jealousy, and pop ideology dominate the panel discussions."

One way his critics get back at him is by calling his work "boring" or "repetitive" or "too demanding." I kept seeing such comments, even from those who in general admire his work. My wife, Jane, suggested we show the films to some children the age of many who appear in *Deaf* and *Blind,* ten to thirteen, and we did. They were utterly taken by what they saw. They scarcely moved. They remained silent. At moments they gasped in admiration or disbelief. All right, they were suburban children going to fine schools, and no strangers to serious assignments pushed by their elders. We gave the films to one of our sons, who had been working with troubled ghetto children. He and they, too, sat still and were held spellbound throughout *Blind* and *Deaf* both. Afterward the boys and girls voiced a flurry of questions, offered a range of lively comments.

Exactly who is "bored" by these films of Wiseman's? Perhaps some of us are offended because as experts or announcers we have been denied employment, refused permission to do what we otherwise do so commonly on television and elsewhere in our national life: make pronouncements, assert our authority, get seen and heard. His are not the neatly packaged, carefully timed productions that feature smooth-speaking narrators and pundits always sure of themselves. For years Wiseman has kept the experts at bay. His films feature only the inhabitants of the particular world he aims to regard closely. He has had no trouble finding so-called average men, women, and children who have a lot to say about this life, about their fate.

Throughout his career Frederick Wiseman has dared explore directly the fullest range of human experience. In film after film he has rendered us as we are—the complexities, ambiguities, ironies, inconsistencies, contradictions that inform our life. He is, really, kin to some of our writers of short fiction, anxious to comprehend through a particular angle of vision our contingent lives: the way we are shaped by institutions, certainly, but the way we may stand up to them, take only so much from them, or find our own ways of breaking free of them. His careful, respectful, persistent regard for plain, ordinary people puts him in the company of writers such as Raymond Carver, Richard Ford, Bobbie Ann Mason, Toni Morrison, James Alan McPherson: storytellers, not social scientists. While sociologists increasingly play with banks of computers and spew an impenetrably mannered, opaque, highfalutin language, and most anthropologists stay resolutely in the Third World, he and his camera attend the contours of our daily life, and in the end, as with fiction, help us better see and hear ourselves—what such films as *Blind* and *Deaf* do so very well, indeed.

So with Nicholas Nixon's efforts up north at the Perkins School. His camera, of course, does not roam, as Wiseman's does, nor is he intent on connecting the seen to the heard. His is, rather, as T. S. Eliot put it, "the still point of the turning world"— particular moments of evocation, suggestion: the revelation of daily truths that are enacted unselfconsciously in the course of lives lived under special circumstances. Wiseman asks us to travel, to take in a narrative breadth he has attended, accumulated, shaped. Nixon insists upon a moment of irony here, a time of surprise there—he offers emblematic instances for us to contemplate in all their instructive singularity. His focused, even confined, scenes paradoxically open the viewer's mind to possibilities and complexities otherwise unimagined, unrecognized. A boy's uplifted face, in profile, his clasped hands, light glowing on them and on the extended neck, the cheek become a gentle hill, the eye socket a valley, and then the brow's foothills of thought—here is a prayerful introspection that has no need of the surrounding human or natural landscape as they get transmitted by the optic nerve. Indeed, in picture after picture human activity and human connection become so sharply defined and confined that we are carried from the visual to the visionary. A youth's fingers on a piano, his hovering head and huddled hulk so close to those keys, tell of sound's commanding, captivating authority: a world to summon with fingers, to explore with one's mind and heart, both. A boy's left hand touching a man's hand as it, in turn, touches his right shoulder, tells of trust earned, of course, but also of race become reduced to the utter irrelevance of pigment—here blindness enables a stirring utopian prophecy.

Someday this kind of color-blind world will grace us, give us the dignity and freedom so long denied us as we have taken our all-too-careful measure of one another with our cruelly alert, encompassing eyes—their competence, in this respect, a death blow to moral worth. A young woman's hand touching her lips, her teeth, seems to be a way of heightening an inward smile, one that makes a nearby landscape a mere shadow of no consequence: the light on a face has its own sources, is independent of nature's whims. With one child after another, actually, the glow of cheek and chin, of nose and, needless to say, eyes, stops us in our readily compassionate tracks, signals a kind of fierce and burning intensity of feeling, a concentrated awareness that draws on what is happening behind a boy's, a girl's countenance rather than outside it. A girl feels her way through a piece of watermelon by touch. Lost to her is the color red, the green of the rind; but surely she knows the various textures and consistencies of that slice of fruit in a way that escapes us—the meat, the seeds, the "skin," each a distinct story for her fingers. Her

right eye looks beyond it all, gives her a distance on food many of us (consumed by it even as we consume it) yearn in vain to achieve. A woman's head touches a child's face, even as the young one's eyes are drawn to the light—and therein so much of what limited vision means: the disconnection that goes with experiencing a hand without taking in, right away, its owner; and the ironic tug of sunshine, which for some partially blind people penetrates the darkness, but only so much. Children savor with tactile interest and enthusiasm a flowering branch, a piece of fruit, a stretch of land with its humble but brave and sturdy native growth, a doll, and, not least, the pages of books. How near the boys and girls draw to those letters and words—those messages near physically and near courtesy of ever responsive hands.

Those hands mean so very much to those youngsters. Walker Percy, in the closing lines of *The Movie-goer,* has his novel's protagonist, Binx Bolling, declare in his usually wry but now determined way, "There is only one thing I can do: listen to people, see how they stick themselves in the world, hand them along a ways in their dark journey and be handed along, and for good and selfish reasons." Such words speak volumes not only for those of us enamored of twentieth-century "existentialism," with its insistence upon our personal struggle for meaning in an often inscrutable world, but for these youths who have learned what Nietzsche had in mind for us to ponder, but, more important, experience: "It takes two to make a truth." Here is that aphorism given the incarnation of two boys utterly engrossed in affirming their humanity through the effort to understand one another—and we are the creature who does just that, through words and symbols, through utterances, we learn from, ask of one another. A girl flexes a finger to touch a thumb—in a gesture an evocation of a skill, of manual dexterity as an instrument of a person's competence, if not agility. Behind those glasses and eyes the brain's cognitive life hums, no matter the sensory "defects" that curb the flow of information from hither and yon to the "I" that is, ultimately, housed in the brain. In several pictures the casual yet often stylized intimacy of these young people is—well, touching. Even as one boy or girl touches another, a measure of trust and need, both, we are very much touched as viewers: an unembarrassed mutuality of being that overcomes the pull toward isolation that blindness and deafness can exert.

Not that some of these children aren't able to fend for themselves quite naturally and comfortably. A girl uses her fingers to count, perhaps, or make a point to herself. Another girl gazes skyward, her lips open invitingly. A third girl fingers a piano's keys with a look of contentment, assurance, even high pleasure. She may need to wear a wide belt to deal with a physical weakness, perhaps of her back, but her tilted face, her glamorously long and fallen hair, her broad smile indicate vitality, an engagement with a muse. A boy clasps his hands, leans a bit on his right shoulder and challenges us to speculate on what crosses his mind—surely nothing too disturbing, because a restful look has spread across his features. Two other boys, in separate pictures, use their hand or hands—one to touch a wall, one as a sort of object of curiosity. These are children trying hard to get their bearings, to contemplate or control the world, to make contact with it, learn its ways, its nature, its responsiveness, to lean upon it, to receive its life—animal, vegetable, mineral. Here words are spoken whispered, music is made, gestures are offered, while a camera makes its record. Here boys and girls come to terms with themselves, their friends and schoolmates, their teachers. Sometimes, as they look askance or into what appear to be indeterminate distances, they seem to be notably reflective beyond their years, intent on an examination of life's meaning rather than its particulars. As we look at them looking, as we remember that, so doing, they may not be seeing something, we are asked, perhaps, to broaden our notion of what it means to try to behold this world, fasten a grip on it, approach it with interest and curiosity and a passion to realize its shapes, its structures, be they man-

made or part of a landscape that is largely untouched by human hands.

When I spent time at the Perkins School with Nicholas Nixon and Bebe Nixon I kept remembering what my father-in-law had told me: that this is the first institution of its kind in America; that it was founded in 1829; that the first director, Samuel Gridley Howe, was a pioneer nineteenth-century reformer and moral leader; that his wife, Julia Ward Howe, authored "The Battle Hymn of the Republic" and herself wanted to make institutional life for the ill, the wayward, the handicapped more decent and honorable; that from 1888 to 1892 Helen Keller and her teacher Anne Sullivan stayed at the school, working together in such a way that both of them would become important educational figures in our country's history. In fact, it was Dickens's references to Perkins in his *American Notes,* which Helen Keller's mother read, that persuaded her to be in contact with an institution far away from Alabama, where she and her daughter lived. Dickens had described the way a blind and deaf girl, Laura Bridgman, had been taught, and eventually Helen Keller's entrance into the world of knowledge and language would itself be a subject of inspiration and reflection—most recently in the essays of the twentieth-century novelist Walker Percy, whose daughter Ann was born deaf.

Today Perkins is in Watertown, and has an impressive campus of mostly Tudor "cottages," as well as an imposing chapel and library in the Gothic tradition. I met students who are blind, who are blind and deaf; I met, too, students who have some sight, but not enough to manage in an ordinary school setting. Each of these students has his or her own medical story, not to mention a chronicle of confusion and anxiety and felt helplessness that, in their sum, have been challenged by a school with a long history of courageous (and ingenious) resistance to such threats to the mind's, the body's survival. "Please talk louder," one blind youth tells me—my anxieties expressing themselves in a mumbling, nasal monotone. Then, a tactful but vigorous explanation: "I want to locate you!" The verb strikes me; I realize that a young woman wants to be sure she has got me precisely placed so that she can correctly send her words in my direction. Put differently, she wants to address me personally, rather than me as an abstraction—a someone somewhere around. Once I am in her line or range of "vision," it might be put, she looks at me directly, continually, talks in a most affecting and unhesitating manner. Later, as I watch her similarly engage with others, show her sensitivity to their every shift in tone, their every bodily move, I think of her as possessed of radar, her blindness unable to deter her from getting a precise sense of who is where, and, too, what is where. She sizes up rooms, takes their measure, maps a given scene, and so negotiates her way rather well in the day-to-day territory she has made her own. I close my eyes, in a gesture of imitation and empathy and emulation, and find myself overwhelmed at the prospect of spending any time in such a "condition." When I open my eyes, I unwittingly answer a question she has put to me in a louder voice—as if I am conscious in a heightened way of her blindness by virtue of my foolishly self-indulgent attempt to simulate her situation for myself. But she is quick to discern the shift in my voice, asks me if I'm all right. She has spotted not only a raised voice but its apprehensiveness. I say I'm fine—but her face registers perplexity, so I think at first, or rather, a sense of worry for me: one more visitor whose normality with respect to his eyes and ears has now been engaged by those who have their own manner of taking in the world, managing in its midst.

The more I feel myself inadequately or hurriedly or nervously trying to keep up with these boys and girls, fit into a mode of engagement they have mastered, the more I doubt my own competence as an observer, a listener. These blind ones can hone in, leave me working hard to be apace with them, even as the deaf ones sign their way to an easy and lively eloquence that leaves me out, worried and nervous and uncomprehending. We all are visitors to one another, of course—in a sense, at the mercy of a neuro-chemistry that makes us or breaks us as one with another, or one with several others. In my first moments at Perkins I felt like the privileged visitor who wanted to "stoop and conquer"—a noblesse oblige that would earn me some documentary evidence: successful "interviews" with "handicapped children." But anyone who has been in the company of blind youths who are reading Braille, or uncannily using sounds to "see," and deaf youths signing (and watching others with all their might as they move and talk), will know the spell of self-doubt I felt, which one of the teachers promptly noticed, hence this brief comment, if not epiphany: "We are humbled by what the children have learned to do. We are always trying to catch up with them—we run after them as much as we try to head them in the right direction!"

Her remarks reminded me of many conversations I had, years earlier, with Anna Freud, whose long-standing interest in, and work with, blind children especially, but also deaf children, attracted much less attention than her other research—for reasons she was not unable or unwilling to consider: "It is hard to put ourselves in the shoes of the blind or the deaf. We use our eyes and ears so constantly, the idea of losing them frightens us badly—it is as though we are losing ourselves! When we get sick, with heart trouble or cancer, we are still ourselves; but were we to go blind or lose our hearing, we'd be cut off, cut down it really is, to a level of isolation that is almost beyond our capacity to imagine. Several of my analytic patients have closed their eyes for long stretches [while lying on her psychoanalytic couch] in order not to be distracted as they let their minds 'go' [free associate], but they would often open them suddenly, just to 'check on things,' one of them kept telling me. I wondered what she had in mind— what she wanted to 'check,' and why. She laughed and said she was afraid that if she didn't do so, she'd get 'lost.' I asked for a further exploration. She replied that she 'quite irrationally' was afraid that her eyes might *stay* closed. 'And then what?' I asked that—and she took a long time replying. Then she said, with a quite flattened voice, and barely audible: 'Why, then—I should be on my way to death.' Immediately I asked her how she felt when she was going to sleep, or, for that matter, awakening. She said 'that's different,' and she knew I'd ask for an explanation, and so she gave one to me—she said that when you go to sleep you are choosing to remove yourself from the world for a stated number of hours; but if you are blind or deaf, you are cut off from others in the course of your awake time, and that leaves you all alone, for her a kind of living death. This was not a surprising notion; many of my patients will come up with a similar line of thought, but I'm afraid they are not getting as close to the nub of the matter as they (and I) would hope!"

For Miss Freud (and her longtime colleague and friend, Dorothy Burlingham), work with blind children (which they both pursued for many years in England) did not prove to be as melancholy as the random thoughts and conjectures of her adult analysands seemed to suggest. When we who are sighted shut our eyes and connect the subsequent darkness we experience with death, we are, of course, linking ourselves with a long cultural tradition that emphasizes the closed lids as external (visual) evidence of a life that has ended—in painting and sculpture such is a clue: we look upon someone who can no longer return that look. Death, then, becomes a matter of complete darkness—as in the phrase "the dead of night." Indeed, what Miss Freud heard from her adult analysands many of us who practice psychoanalytic psychiatry hear again and again—the eyes as a witness not only of objects, but of life itself. Here one need only let one's mind wander across an entire symbolic landscape—the sun's light as life-giving, the evening's darkness as the opposite. Black moods contrast with the white heat of creativity—and on and on the weighted language goes.

As a matter of fact, when I was talking with African-American youths in Atlanta, as they initiated school desegregation in the 1960s, I kept hearing references to skin color that had far wider implications—as in this excerpt from an extended conversa-

tion with a sixteen-year-old young woman who, with only one other person of her race, was at school with a thousand or so white youths: "They keep looking at me as if I'm going to harm them somehow. They don't want to go near me. My daddy told me—'They'll think you'll get them sick, that's how their minds work,' and he's right, but it's worse than that. It's as if everything will end for 'them' if a few of 'us' come and stay here. There's this one girl who's white, and she and I have become friends; she's the only one who will do that with me. We gab together in the girl's room, and she's very smart, and she tells me that the white folks are plain scared of us, the colored people, and I should remember that, because they're trying to make *me* scared, when it's *them*—they're the ones [who are scared]. All right, I told her, maybe she's right, but what are they scared of, that's what I'd like to know. Well, she said, you hear all these awful swear words, the ignorant 'white trash' talk; but she said she has a friend, and she's not mean, and she doesn't hate the Negro people, but she said that they're different, that's what she told my white friend; and she asked how, why—what's the difference? Her friend said that when she stops and *thinks*, she knows there *isn't* any difference, other than skin color, but she has to admit that it's more than that in her mind, it's like—it's the difference between the morning, when you're wide awake and full of plans, and late at night, when all you want to do is fall asleep. But it's silly to think like that, her friend admitted, and my friend just laughed and said it goes to show you how silly all this prejudice talk is."

When I heard those words I paid them little heed. I was interested in the way this young person was handling the severe strain of dealing with the marked isolation that was her daily fate. The random thoughts, conveyed secondhand, of an anonymous white youth seemed altogether unsurprising and all too familiar: prejudice wears many faces, all of them scowling. But later, when I showed the transcripts of a number of interviews with a number of African-American children to my friend and adviser, the psychoanalyst Erik H. Erikson, in whose course I had become a section leader, he put a check mark beside the above segment of that young woman's statement, and suggested we discuss it. I wasn't sure why he picked those remarks, but soon enough would learn why: "That [white] girl does sound like 'any old bigot,' you might call her. But I think her words 'stuck' to her friend's mind, and you'll notice [that] she made sure she repeated what she heard to the Negro girl. I'm sure she's heard lots of not very nice descriptions of Negro people, but *that* one—you see, she somehow 'had' to share with this new friend she's made at school. To my mind the idea of the morning belonging to white people and the evening belonging to Negroes is not an unusual one—and you and I can let our psychoanalytic minds sort out various 'associations' implied in that distinction. Negroes are so often called names that imply dirt or sexuality (or both, linked)—all a part of our 'darker' life. White people are 'cleaner,' 'purer,' 'higher,' in their thinking and their lives: the children of light and the children of darkness! But this girl is pushing all that well-known symbolism a little further. She is saying that we *live* in the day, we *die* at night—even as that would come as a surprise to many 'night owls,' and, of course, couples have sex, usually (or so it is thought!) at night. Conventional psychological wisdom tells us that the Negro is feared and then hated because he stands for the forbidden or the desired (or both)—which whites reject: the Negro as a scapegoat, the one who receives insults from people eager to dump on others what they can't tolerate knowing is 'alive and well' in themselves! But I think that that girl was pushing us to think about darkness as death, and light as life, and I'll bet if we could pursue that theme, that 'polarity' with her, we'd find more about what happens to us when we think about death, what it means to us."

With that, Erikson closed his eyes, and upon opening them, a mere second or two later, he asked me to take notice of that involuntary act, as he saw it: you see, I've just shut myself off, for the briefest time, from this room, from you, from all that is here,

around me and familiar and pleasant. I could tell you that I was 'thinking for a minute,' but I wasn't really. I withdrew into silent darkness, and nothing at all crossed my mind! That's a small death, maybe—if we're to pursue this [line of inquiry]. I'm not sure I wasn't 'acting' for myself, showing myself and you what that girl might have had in mind; but this is *so* complicated: it requires a full-length, extended investigation!"

On to other matters we went—but a year later that discussion would weigh heavily on my mind as I sat with Anna Freud for the first time in an office supplied her at Yale, where she was doing some lecturing and research. We stumbled into the subject of blindness by accident. She had asked me about the teaching I was doing and I told her about the novel I was using in a new course I'd just got going. When I mentioned *Invisible Man* she got curious; she'd not heard of it, but the title intrigued her. She assumed the story had "something to do with the unseen"—and, of course, she laughed upon saying that, and told me she wasn't "very well versed" in modern literature (the novel had been published only fifteen years earlier). I gave her a relatively brief synopsis, told her that the protagonist's invisibility as a Negro (the word then used by people like me) bespoke of a blindness in those who didn't seem able to "see" him in any knowing, full, respectful way. I can still hear her in my head (as well as on my tape recorder, if I so choose!) saying, "Oh, blindness—that is a big subject!" She went further, and so I asked her if she'd ever "worked with a blind patient." Yes, she had—and then, a wonderfully instructive description of her interest in blind children, and an explanation of her reasons. When I told her of the above moment in Erik Erikson's office in Harvard's Widener Library, she smiled and averred that she didn't disagree with the "tenor" of our discussion, and that she especially agreed with her former analysand (she was Erikson's training analyst in Vienna in the late 1920s, early 1930s) that blindness is a "quite complex matter," one she was "getting to understand only gradually."

I fear I was all too rashly willing to share my

understanding of that "complex matter"; and I did so by telling her stories I'd come to know in the course of my work with children from various social and racial backgrounds. She listened with the great tact and intense attention characteristic of her at all times, and thanked me for helping her to understand how race blinds people to what is so evidently there, waiting to be appreciated, or, better, seen: "It is true that a person can get carried away by racism; but I'm not sure 'blindness' is the right word for what happens. The person is seen [an African-American, say], but through a certain lens—a distorting lens. In a way, you know, a racist sees himself when he sees a Negro and starts calling him all those unkind words and phrases! Our [psychoanalytic] word 'projection' fits the bill—it describes what happens when we get rid of qualities we don't like by pinning them on someone else. Now, you will agree, I think, that to do so requires some 'looking'—you have to pick the 'right' person for your hateful blaming, for your critical attention. I know I am quibbling here with you—I know what you're trying to say, that many white people ignore the Negro, don't see Negroes as individuals, but as *Negroes,* first and last and always; and I do understand why you would want to call such people 'blind.' There *is* a kind of blindness in operation there—things are being overlooked or ignored, so that the bigot can feel satisfied with himself at the expense of someone else. The bigot, I guess we should say, to be exact, is someone who is first blind to himself, then blind about certain others. When you used that phrase 'see through' to describe what happens to the 'invisible man,' you were saying a lot; you were telling me what I'm trying to tell you! [I had noted that various characters in the Ellison novel 'saw right through him, as if he didn't really exist as an individual.'] A bigot does just that, 'sees through' those selected for contempt. But to 'see through' is to see in a certain way. To be blind is not to see—and there is where I start in my research: I'm trying to learn from blind children what goes on as they get through their days."

At that point, alas, I tried to show Miss Freud how clever I was. I seized upon her word "days," pointed out that such children probably didn't know the difference between day and night. She smiled, very delicately shook her head, told me that she had also surmised as much at the start of her research, but had been "asked" to change her mind by the children—not a formal request, she hastened to let me know (I had asked her about that word "asked"), but as a consequence of what she had learned from the boys and girls whose sustained and close acquaintance she had made. A few minutes later, as she was describing some of those children, she ventured ever so cautiously into the realm of the conceptual, with this statement: "The blind don't 'see' what we think they see—'darkness,' or so I've come to think on the basis of what I've heard from my teachers, these few young ones I've been meeting. When I ask them what is on their minds when they are alone, or when they are sitting with me, I am told that so-and-so is on this boy's mind, and that someone else is on that girl's mind. I am told that the child is listening to something that's been said, that's remembered—and, of course, my 'regular' adult analysands will tell me the same thing: 'I just thought of something that my mother once told me,' and I'll be informed that the patient is now 'hearing' the mother's voice saying what I've just been informed was spoken! We who see remember seeing people, and their images also fill our minds; but for those who have never had eyes that work, there are plenty of voices to recall, and, also, experiences of touching others and being touched. A blind child told me, 'I can remember my mother holding my hand—I was little, and she made sure that I never bumped into anything, and I never fell down. She was amazing, she did it all silently—guiding me with a nudge, or tapping my shoulder or my arm, or putting her arm around me for a "teeny second," she'd say, and she lived up to her words.' You can see what I have in *my* mind—the voices of the children I've chosen to get to know!"

She stopped to sip the coffee she prepared for both of us. She and I were both aware that we were "look-conscious"—quite mindful that a pair of sharp eyes were instrumental in enabling some fancy tea cups and saucers to be used, not to mention an electric coffeemaker. As she proceeded, I spoke—mentioned how hard it would be for someone blind to go through the motions as she had just done. True, but she had seen blind children prepare food and drink for themselves and others. They had been "led through certain steps" by a teacher, and had soon enough mastered them. Now, with some coffee in her, she wanted to say more: "At first I wondered if blindness didn't really cut the children off, make them really (and literally!) withdrawn from the world. I realized, as I've just said, that a child in a good school, where a staff knows how to work with the blind—that child will learn to manage quite well, because he's being taught, patiently, to do things, to rely on others, and to rely on himself, or herself, as the case may be!

"In time, I shifted my emphasis—I wasn't so interested any longer in the 'mechanical' side of the children's lives: how they get to do things, how they are *taught* to do things. I wanted to learn about how their minds worked, what happened to them emotionally. A big clue came to me one day from a ten-year-old girl. I was asking her how she spent her days, what she liked to do and what she didn't at all enjoy doing, and she suddenly became quite forcefully didactic with me. She said, 'Miss Freud, I do what I please!' Well, I was taken by surprise. She had seemed like such an easygoing and gracious child, and here she was being quite—how do you say it in America?—quite 'full of herself.' Now, she heard my silence, and so she continued, good instructor that she was! She reminded me of the obvious, that she wasn't at the beck and call of the world, the way sighted people are. She had voices calling her out of herself, but not sights of various sorts. She was, thereby, quite naturally cut off—and so she told me when she said words to this effect: 'I sit and think about what happened to me, last week or the week before. I sit and wonder what will happen next month. I feel nice and cozy and comfortable, just being there, and realizing that I'm me, and I'll keep

being me for a long time. I take my pulse. I can feel my heart beating. I hear me breathing in and breathing out. I feel my foot moving on the floor—my socks are on, but my shoes are off! I hold my hands together and I cross my legs. Then I let my hands hang loose, and I uncross my legs. I like to feel my hair a lot—it's soft and I shake it and I run my hands through it. There's lots to do—all I want to do, I just do!'

"She'd given *me* 'lots to do'—to contemplate! I now was beginning to understand that she hadn't been some 'spoiled child,' who is 'stuck on herself'; no, she is—I guess you could say 'stuck *in* herself,' a little more so, at least, than the many of us."

A thin smile, so familiar to those who knew her, came upon a face hitherto earnestly serious. Now we had left the subject of "blindness" and were right smack in the middle of the subject of psychoanalytic theory, its helpful, suggestive possibilities on the one hand, but, on the other, its temptations, none more beguiling (and dangerous) than that of the categorization wielded in the name of clear-cut differentiations and definitions, as in the blind are *this,* the deaf are *that.* Anna Freud was letting me know about a kind of narcissism: the relatively enveloped world of a child who goes undistracted by eyes that take in the endless pictorial scenes to which each of us, all the time, is heir. But she knew that there are plenty of narcissists around whose eyes are in no way clouded, let alone thoroughly unresponsive to the constant stimuli offered us "normal" ones when we are awake and going about our day's or evening's business. Still, she wanted to consider "the overall picture," as she would put it: the particular invitations or discouragements that befall the blind—setting the stage for a corresponding set of adaptive reactions. She had noticed the way blind children, even ones not shy, but, rather, outgoing, have to struggle hard and long to resist the satisfactions of the self, the "I" that, relatively undistracted, takes continuing notice of itself, its mind and body alike. The eyes, after all, connect us quite constantly with what exists or is happening outside ourselves. Without the eyes, there are the ears, needless to say—though at the Perkins School and the Alabama Institute for the Blind and Deaf there are children who are both blind and deaf. There is also the vast territory known as the skin, that semipermeable membrane that both protects us and allows for contact between us and others, not to mention us and a neighborhood's physicality. (Taste and smell are available to us, but unlike, say, our dogs, the nose or the tongue doesn't transmit the kind of commanding messages that the other senses can muster.) Still, notwithstanding those other avenues of connection with the outside world, when a youngster can't see, the "self" is more than incited to reconnoiter within its own territory, hence the "withdrawn" or "inward" children one can see at Perkins or its sister/brother institution in Alabama, which I so remember visiting.

There in the South, actually, a teacher who had worked with blind and deaf children (not to mention a few both blind and deaf) reminded me that blind children who have good hearing are less drawn to voices than the rest of us, because they lack the ability to attach spoken words to someone's visual presence, and, as a result, are less stirred or "turned on" by what they hear. A look of doubt on my face (speaking of a "visual presence"!) was directly countered with this advisory rejoinder: "Close your eyes for a long time, and talk with people and see if it's the same." I remained skeptical—until I got to talk with a young man who had been able to see until he was seven or eight, whereupon a rare ophthalmological disorder ensued. He vividly recalled for me the transition that took place within him: "Not being able to look at who was talking to me made a big difference—I can think back and remember how it started to happen, the difference. I began to lose interest in a lot of what people said to me, especially strangers. I mean, the people I could remember seeing, I saw while they talked to me, my mom and daddy and my brothers and my sister, and my momma [grandmother]; but with new folks, it wasn't the same listening. I think I know how a lot of the kids here feel [who have never experienced any

degree of visual competence]. You can get them to hear you, and they'll pay you good attention, but it's not the same 'buzz' you get when there's the one, before you, who's saying something, and you can take her right in with your eyes, or the guy."

The eyes as instruments of the absorption that he has mentioned: "taking in" the human scene, the hereabouts of *this* place or *that* one. In the Perkins School I "took in" children thoroughly "independent," a casual observer might conclude, and so they were; but they might also have been regarded as insistently aloof, even in the face of the moments and longer of reliance they had to place in certain others, those who taught and cared for them in a residential setting that allows for a person-to-person kind of instruction. Had I not met some children, years earlier in Alabama, similarly trying to make do in the face of the obstacles fate had put in their paths, and had I not heard Anna Freud attempting (with admitted difficulty) to figure out the complexity of things—how refreshing, in that regard, her candor—I am certain I would have been even more at a loss as I tried to connect with these children, themselves at a loss. As it was, I was most grateful for the kindness and patience of the boys and girls I met, who knew well that they were being observed, and who knew rather readily how to go about their business without any great self-consciousness—maybe the precise point: whereas at the Tobin School or Boston Latin School a visitor could incite various expressions of heightened awareness (furtive glances, a shyness or its opposite, a performer's zeal), these children, by and large, had their own agendas to pursue with a comparative (and ironic) self-sufficiency that told its own story.

In that regard, I will long keep in mind what I heard from a somewhat sullen blind boy—so I described him to myself, I suppose to protect my own pride as I felt him giving me very little attention, and, maybe as well, to take the kind of (psychological) swipe at him that people like me have learned to find all too available under certain circumstances. I had asked this youngster (he was about ten or eleven) "how it goes"—that vague bit of polite inquiry that, one hopes, will earn a more than mono-syllabic answer, and that, with any luck, can some-times elicit a valuable train of thought. But all to no effect: "It goes," I hear. I feel rebuffed, but remember the resilience I've encountered in so many children, and, too, the presumptuousness that can inform the questions posed, and posed to people who, after all, have their own lives to live, with obligations and responsibilities that may elude a person who wants them to stop and totally take stock in the interests of something called "research." I try to slip into pleas-ant banter, but get nowhere, and rather quickly am told, "I've got to go."

I feel rebuffed, naturally, and my face shows it. The teacher standing near me waits for the child to leave, then tells me not to take what happened per-sonally. I nod. I know she is right. She takes advan-tage, then, of this moment—tells me that some of the children at the school are inevitably "quite shut off," don't easily engage with others, especially peo-ple they have never before met. Yes, I say, and that can be the case with certain children in any school; they are quite simply (or not so simply) shy. True, she allows, but for blind boys and girls each new person is not met the way the rest of us take in one another: a glance, a more sustained look, a glare even. Then, a bit of interpretation or advice for me: "You speak quietly. With some of our children, it's best to speak up, to reach out to them with your voice, show them that you're eager to be with them. They make their judgments, remember, by what they hear. If you're reserved—well, they'll be guarded, too."

I am beginning to understand, courtesy of such a lesson, how "it goes," as the boy just put it, for him: sound rather than sight as the first, testing connec-tion—and the requirement for me to come to terms not only with the somewhat distanced "self" of a child, but with my own self's manner of relating to others. When Miss Freud had spoken of the particu-lar form of "narcissism" one often finds in blind (or deaf) children, she wasn't name-calling—or denying that "narcissism" to the rest of us. We all have our-selves as our rock-bottom possession—a place where

we live, which we inhabit, try to uphold and defend, and with pleasure or pain (or a mix of the two) pre-sent to others, who reciprocate. Much of that human engagement takes place through the eyes: we size one another up, even as we prepare (and preen) our-selves in advance for such moments. Then sound kicks in—the words we use, the way we use them, and the gestures we make to help them, as it were, hit home: come across to another convincingly. To subtract from such a self-presentation by eliminating vision or hearing makes for a challenge not only for the child at Perkins, but his or her teachers (or visi-tors). How well are we sighted ones prepared to make the accommodations and initiatives that will help not only the students, but ourselves? In Miss Freud's technical language, once used by both of us (back and forth we went, speaking of narcissism: the-oretical talk as a means of mutual comprehension, if not plain showing off!), "The narcissism of the blind requires an adaptive narcissism in their caretakers" (not to mention psychoanalytic observers).

Similarly for the deaf, as I also began to realize at the Perkins School. Now the eyes work overtime, attempting (through "signing") to engage the person with others, and, obviously, as a necessary part of lin-guistic exchange—to the point that the briefest clo-sure of the eyes, or distraction of them (a sidelong look, a gaze that distracts) turns into a refusal: "Our [deaf] children have their very own ways of being polite or unfriendly," a teacher tells me, not to make a psychological generalization about "the deaf," but to connect their humanity to ours, to hers and all those who attend the children at school. The child who has prompted that remark by casting a glance toward the window, thereby stopping a conversation cold, also has "reduced vision," though she obviously can see a good deal more of the world than many at the school who see nothing at all. The cliché that each of us is different takes on a new meaning for me under such circumstances—the realization, for instance, that a shadowy world can mean a lot, as compared to one that cannot be glimpsed at all.

I sit and watch children at the Perkins School read by Braille: I note their busy, committed absorption of words. Like millions of readers across the planet, they are drinking knowledge, and occasionally, wisdom. My memory carries me back to a discussion I had years earlier with one of Anna Freud's psychoanalytic colleagues, who also worked with blind children. It is those fingers, working so busily, effectively that prompt the memory. I'd been told by that psychoanalyst of a child who kept worrying that her fingers would "freeze," and that she'd no longer be able to read. A not very surprising kind of anxiety or fear for a blind girl to have, in the midst of her education—so I would only really understand when I'd watched children learning in this way, with their hands rather than their eyes. Until that time, I'd not extended my imagination enough to think about the manner in which such young people express the inevitable worries (in all of us) that accompany schooling. At Perkins I could readily conceive of deaf children rubbing their eyes with alarm, before an exam, or blind children flexing their fingers worriedly before the teacher gets ready to ask questions. "Once you have worked with the children here, you can anticipate what the problems will be," a young teacher tells me—the purest of common sense, of course, but each of us has his or her common sense to acquire. Just after those words were spoken, the teacher saw a possible disagreement brewing between two children, and she left me for a more immediate attentiveness toward the two girls: she put her right hand on one girl's shoulder, her left hand on the other girl's shoulder, and said one word, "please," firmly yet as a request rather than a demand. It seemed to me that a calm settled on the two girls, and on their teacher: this I saw, and this those three felt through touch. Only one word was used—a humbling moment for one who uses so many words in his life as a doctor, teacher, writer!

To touch—not so easy for some of us who try to teach or heal to contemplate without evident (and necessary) concern. The photographs of children at Perkins show touching as a near constant, a natural part of the school's everyday fare. That is, learning is done through touching (Braille), and people get along through the affirmations and constraints that touching can enable. I begin to realize, eventually, the new possibilities that even the conventional handshake can offer. The children linger with their handshakes, be they firm or flaccid—testing the waters, taking in one another through touch before there is talk. Interestingly, I note that I am looking at those handshakes, even as the children direct their unseeing eyes toward my face, even as their faces, in respective ways, register this moment of relatedness. Perhaps my eyes have come to understand the futility of customary eye contact; or perhaps those eyes have realized where contact is really taking place between me and a child, and so have learned to travel there. Meanwhile, the children can take such a highly charged encounter for granted, hence their (relative) "cool" about what is transpiring. Meanwhile, too, I am discovering that my hands as well as my voice have some learning to accomplish. Even as the teachers gently encourage me to "speak up," to offer my voice more forthrightly, generously, to these children, I am also becoming painfully aware of how restrained and aloof I am with respect to my body, my hands, as I stand here or there, watching and listening and trying to link myself through words and (feeble) gestures to these youths whose hungers and thirsts with respect to the world are no different in many respects than mine, though the way they apprehend that world does indeed present for them challenges unknown to me. I catch myself wondering hard about that word "apprehend," a resort to the analytic sensibility: the children live up to that word in its literal sense—affirm its derivation, to take hold of something. But I also catch hold of *myself;* a feeling of apprehension comes over me as I observe what Nicholas Nixon's pictures show so, yes, touchingly: students and teachers touching one another, brushing up against one another, caressing one another, an expressiveness of the flesh that gets to me, that unnerves me, hence *my* version of that word "apprehend"—I take note of what is taking place and, so doing, become "apprehensive," meaning that what I have apprehended has stirred me a good deal.

No wonder, such being the case, I sought the sanction of Anna Freud! When in doubt, in felt jeopardy, turn to your parents, your teachers, some mixture of the two that you have come to realize in a person who thereby truly matters to you. Had she not once told me of her own difficulties in working with blind children—"the special parameters one has to use," meaning (less formally, more personally), the efforts of outreach necessary: that outreach become a voice newly charged, a hand more relaxed in its availability, and one's body able to serve others appropriately rather than exploitatively. I realize those last two adverbs can each be the occasion of a long discussion—and not only in connection with the students at the Perkins School; but even the most cursory of visits there (or visits with this book's pictures) will bring such words to mind: how to touch others in truly the right way, with the right spirit?

One morning, when I left the Perkins School, I kept remembering a remark my mother used to make—that "the eyes are the windows of the soul." One of her sentimental, quasi-religious statements of a kind my scientist dad often patronized as an "amusing way of putting things." She was probably telling us that in some fashion we reveal ourselves wordlessly to others by the way we look (at them, at others), and, in the colloquial sense, by our looks (both our general appearance and our manner of eyeing people, animals, the physical setting near at hand). What, then, of these children at Perkins—how to get some entry to *their* soul's nature? I found their faces sometimes inviting, welcoming, or, alas, inaccessible, and in that regard, forbidding—even as such is the case with all of us: some of our faces reach out, touch others; some of our faces scowl, withdraw from anyone's scrutiny, however well intentioned, even affectionate. "Truth comes in degrees," I once luckily heard the poet and physician William Carlos Williams say after a lecture, when he was pestered by someone who wanted flatout, cement wall–thick distinctions with respect to "artists," "creativity," and such words that, alas, some of us want to reserve for a few (ourselves and our various buddies, companions). He would have no part of it, a question that was meant to split people

so decisively, definitively, hence his aphoristic reply, intended to cut the advance (the assault) at the pass. His face glowered, we all saw; and those of us who were lucky to know him understood well how hard he was working, with the help of those four words, carefully chosen, to keep his annoyance (and more) under wraps—he who, in *Paterson,* blasted away repeatedly at those who claim for themselves, the proverbial precious few, certain special privileges of mind, heart, soul. So, still driving my car away from Perkins, but very much *there,* yet, in my head, I summon my old teacher, Dr. Williams, to help me sort matters out, gain some entry into certain souls without resorting to exaggeration or distortion, without a loss of context. Suddenly, through Dr. Williams's "eyes," as it were, I "see" what Nicholas Nixon's pictures, actually, reveal to us, tell us in their vivid, arresting "moments": the blind nevertheless have "eyes" (faces, a manner of being) that are, indeed, as marvelously revelatory as my mom told us hers or ours or anyone's could be (or inadvertently are). Put differently, blindness in and of itself will not deprive this or that child of his or her humanity, in all its possibilities. For any blind boy or girl "truth" also "comes in degrees"—the complex variousness of a particular life.

Finally, still in the car, but nearer home, I wander from W. C. Williams to a storyteller who greatly admired him (and even wrote a poem in which he said so)—Raymond Carver, whose fiction, like Williams's poetry, I keep pressing on my students, on myself. Carver's great story "Cathedral" treats of a trio, a middle-aged couple and a visitor who comes to spend a holiday with them; and he is blind. Out of this threesome (the subtleties of their carryings-on, the shifts in their attitudes and allegiances) a writer has wrought a powerfully instructive moral fable, culminating in an extraordinary scene, wherein the blind man and his host, the husband, who has earlier on been resentful of (unable to fathom) his wife's interest in, friendship with, this stranger, now become together engaged in drawing a cathedral. (They are watching—hearing—a television program that tells of the medieval age, and the construction of such giant churches over the decades, the generations.) Soon enough it is for them a matter of hand on hand, a wondrously affecting shared effort: an expedition or pilgrimage, really, into an understanding that links these individuals, as in Nietzsche's "it takes two to make a truth." Now one does not impart knowledge, the other receive it; now it is "the blind leading the blind"—the leveling of their common humanity, with plenty of "darkness" and limitation for each to bear as a burden, but less so in the other's trusted company.

"Blinded, you fall into darkness, and you're dead"—a statement that pushes things to the limit, so a high school student of mine aimed to do, when he spoke those words, he who had 20/20 vision, and prized his powerful body in a neighborhood where he needed every ounce of strength he had, and, too, an eagle-eyed vision. "Without my eyes working overtime, I'm a goner," he once pointed out—and then he amplified: "I'd not know what I need to know—*everything!* A guy who wanted to knock me out and not face a murder rap, he'd go for my eyes!" So it went, too, in Sophocles' time: you can get to know "everything," but still you're in line for the biggest trouble possible, short of death; and so, Oedipus loses his eyesight—a living death, of sorts, for him, as for a contemporary youth. Yet, the Hebrew prophets and Jesus, who very much espoused their ethics, knew irony, and allowed for forgiveness, a redemptive turn in things. As a consequence, blindness moved from being a terrible curse inflicted on the worst of the worst, those who violate (through acquired knowledge) the most important psychological and moral taboos, to an aspect of our waywardness, our flawed condition, that is around any corner for any of us to meet, come to experience. Under these terms of our personal, our spiritual condition, we have enough in common with any outcasts to warrant a tragic guardedness when we consider them—as in the self-admonition: there but for the grace of God go I.

Today, in a secular society, we speak of the uncon-

scious, that great leveler, as the repository in every single person of all crimes, huge and relatively minor, from incest and murder to a laziness that falls short of sloth, or a silent envy that never springs to enacted greed. For Carver, "Cathedral" was a means of evoking a topsy-turvy Judeo-Christian tradition that warned against moral or psychological self-assurance—a sure prelude to smugness. Christ's closeness to the "despised and scorned" becomes a blind man's affiliation with a heretofore callous American "Joe" who, at the end of this quite plain and funny, but also brilliantly plotted, wondrously narrated short fiction, has turned into a near Tolstoyan sojourner, almost within grasp of a transcendent wisdom, all courtesy of a plain, unaffected blind man whose greatest virtue, courtesy of his creator, is to be thoroughly earthy, a bit naive, and only reluctantly a touch didactic—at his best an accidental moment's spiritual journeyman, only half awake to the mission of sorts that has befallen him, rather than been sought by him.

As I turn off the car's ignition, pick up some "development office" folders graciously given me by a high-up official at the Perkins School (a friend, it turns out, of my wife's family), I settle for Raymond Carver's vision, his view, his insight—all those eye-connected words, even as "eye" and "I" are indistinguishable to our ears except in the context of a sentence, a statement; and it is context that matters, says Carver, in the course of fulfilling his modestly anecdotal calling of the storyteller. No question, to be literally blind is far from fun; but to be blind to others in the subjective or moral sense of that expression is a darkness all its own. At home with Nicholas Nixon's rescued artifacts, which we call photographs (enabled by months of immersion in a school's various rooms), I lower my own eyes, let my mind conjure up Carver's characters and scenes, call them a most helpful guide to an understanding of the altogether frail inwardness in each of us as we stumble along, singing and crying, through our allotted time, unseeing so often, then all of a sudden, clear, at least, about the next step needed.

Illustrations

Perkins School for the Blind

Acknowledgments

My sort of photography could never get off the ground without the collaboration and inspiration of the people who let me take their pictures. So, to the students at Perkins; to the students at Boston Latin; and, because they put up with me every day for a year, to the students of room 306 in the Tobin School—by name: Ashley, Dana, Christa, Molly, Lucien, Marc, Kim, Shavonne, Julia, Genita, Eddie, Rebecca, Greg, Jocelyn, Tammy, Matisse, Jonah, Sarah, Gene, Robey, and Sam—go my biggest thanks, my deepest gratitude.

There were also adults at each school whose generosity and belief in my work made this project possible. At the Tobin School in Cambridge, teacher Chris Affleck, the fertile climate of her room, and her openness to me really began it all; thanks to her, I still think of being eleven years old and in her fifth-grade class as a kind of perfect time. Don Watson, Tobin's principal, and Tim O'Connor, the teaching assistant in room 306, were extraordinarily helpful, supportive, and kind to me daily.

At Perkins School for the Blind, Harry Colt, the director of development, was the man I had to convince and who then made everything possible—and wonderfully. Teacher Denise Fitzgerald became my friend as she helped me to really see the Perkins students more clearly. Bill Brower, Larry Melander, and school director Kevin Lessard provided access, support, and encouragement all the time, and I thank them heartily.

At Boston Latin School, Ron Gwiazda, assistant to the headmaster, was almost as necessary to the process as my camera was. Gwiazda is a hero to me; his kindness, fierce intelligence, and absolute commitment inspired and enabled me like a beautiful day. Teachers Jack Regan, Ruthann Kelley, Chuck Aversa, Marianne Pagos, Catherine Wight, Shari Lewis, Roseanna Fernandez, Monique Brun, Nancy O'Malley, and Chris Idzik repeatedly opened their doors to my hardly invisible process. Michael Contompasis, the headmaster, let me see how a real leader guides: with absolute dedication, high principle, and courtesy, all as real as they get.

I am honored to thank Robert Coles for his true understanding of and affection for what I have tried to do. His work has been most important to me for years, and to do this with him is like being a second baseman behind Nolan Ryan. Thank you, Bob. I also wish to thank Richard Phillips, who made the splendid camera with which all these pictures were taken.

My family—Bebe, Sam, and Clem—is in all of these pictures. They inspire me, challenge me, and put up with me, and I would be in jail or in a camera club without their love for me. And mine for them.

—Nicholas Nixon